case studies in
ARCHAEOLOGY

SERIES EDITOR
JEFFREY QUILTER
Washington, DC

THE PITHOUSES OF

KEATLEY CREEK

COMPLEX HUNTER–GATHERERS

OF THE NORTHWEST PLATEAU

THE PITHOUSES OF
KEATLEY CREEK
COMPLEX HUNTER–GATHERERS
OF THE NORTHWEST PLATEAU

BRIAN HAYDEN
Simon Fraser University

WADSWORTH

™

THOMSON LEARNING

Wadsworth/Thomson Learning
10 Davis Drive
Belmont, CA 94002-3098
USA

For information about our products, contact us:
Thomson Learning Academic Resource Center
1-800-423-0563
http://www.wadsworth.com

International Headquarters
Thomson Learning
International Division
290 Harbor Drive, 2nd Floor
Stamford, CT 06902-7477
USA

UK/Europe/Middle East/South Africa
Thomson Learning
Berkshire House
168-173 High Holborn
London WCIV 7AA

Asia
Thomson Learning
60 Albert Street, #15-01
Albert Complex
Singapore 189969

Canada
Nelson Thomson Learning
1120 Birchmount Road
Toronto, Ontario MIK 5G4
Canada
United Kingdom

ISBN 0-534-44186-6

The Adaptable Courseware Program consists of products and additions to existing Wadsworth Group products that are produced from camera-ready copy. Peer review, class testing, and accuracy are primarily the responsibility of the author(s).

To Desmond Peters Sr.
Stl'alt'imx tradition bearer

FOREWORD

ABOUT THE SERIES

These case studies in archaeology are designed to bring students in beginning and intermediate courses in archaeology, anthropology, history, and related disciplines insights into the theory, practice, and results of archaeological investigations. They are written by scholars who have had direct experience in archaeological research, whether in the field, laboratory, or library. The authors are also teachers, and in writing their books they have kept the students who will read them foremost in their minds. These books are intended to present a wide range of archaeological topics as case studies in a form and manner that will be more accessible than writings found in articles or books intended for professional audiences, yet at the same time preserve and present the significance of archaeological investigations for all.

ABOUT THE AUTHOR

Brian Hayden was born on Valentine's Day, 1946, in Flushing, Long Island. Growing up in New Jersey provided many opportunities for fossil hunting in suburban construction sites and for exploring various facets of the region's natural history. While an undergraduate student at the University of Colorado, the allure of prehistoric archaeology was increased through the author's participation in David Breternitz's memorable field camps at Dinosaur National Monument. Both the outdoor adventure of Colorado and the intrigue of dealing with problems of the prehistoric past in the area were critical factors in his pursuit of a career in archaeology.

Subsequently, he worked as a field assistant in Tunisia with Gordon Hewes; in Guatemala with William Sanders on the Kaminaljuyu Project; with Joe Ben Wheat and Marie Wormington at the Jurgen's site in Colorado; with Bruce Schroeder in Lebanon; and with Francois Bordes in France. Hayden directed his own projects in Australia where he studied the use of stone tools by Aborigines; in Ontario, where he studied undisturbed Iroquoian houses at the Draper site; and in Mexico and Guatemala where he studied the contemporary material culture of Highland Maya Indians.

Over the past 12 years, Hayden has directed the Fraser River Investigations into Corporate Group Archaeology (FRICGA) project, reported on in this volume, and has begun an ethnoarchaeological study of feasting in Southeast Asia. The guiding principle in all these projects has been the application of cultural ecology to the present and past, an approach strongly advocated by Rolf Knight (then at the University of Toronto) and William Sanders. Hayden's graduate degrees are from the University of Toronto.

Among his numerous books and articles, the following are of particular note: *Archaeology: The science of once and future things; Paleolithic reflections; The structure of material systems* (with Aubrey Cannon); *Nimrods, piscators, pluckers, and planters: The emergence of food production; Big man, big heart? A Mesoamerican view of the emergence of complex society* (with Rob Gargett); and *The cultural capacities of Neandertals: A review and re-evaluation.*

ABOUT THIS CASE STUDY

This slim volume on archaeology at Keatley Creek provides the reader with a wealth of information on a number of important topics. Professor Hayden presents a fascinating view into a little known culture area, demonstrates the power of careful excavation and analyses, offers an intriguing interpretation of the origins of social complexity, and links the archaeological past with the ethnographic present.

The Plateau Culture Region stretches from interior British Colombia through Washington State, into Oregon and Idaho. It was and is a world unto itself, of spectacular beauty, as Brian Hayden's photographs dramatically show. Human occupation was early, intensive, and contoured to the riches and challenges of the natural environment. Despite these wonders, however, archaeological investigations of the area and the interest of the educated public have lagged behind other regions. But, with luck, this excellent book may help to change this situation and bring renewed interest to the land, its people, and its past.

Rough diamonds only shine through the work of skilled cutters. In the case of Keatley Creek, Brian Hayden is its master craftsman. He has devoted many years to careful excavation and analysis of the site, and a great strength of this book is the way in which he is able to clearly show not only the analytical methods used to retrieve and study data but also the reasoning behind such approaches to the archaeological record. He uses both sophisticated techniques and sophisticated thinking in the employment and interpretation of advanced analyses. Readers of this book will gain much in both inspiration and potential perspiration. Meticulous investigation requires patience, fortitude, and plain hard work.

Careful and detailed labor yields high dividends. We learn of the ways in which roof tops were used, where people sat on them, how layers of refuse on the roofs may be interpreted, how their patterns of collapse reveal patterns of abandonment and reuse, to cite but one example. This and other rewards of careful methodology have been used to build an intriguing case to argue the nature and origins of social complexity among the ancient dwellers of the Fraser River Valley. Professor Hayden's theory of the role of aggrandizers in the origins of social complexity will offer much for discussions on the causes of social change and hierarchies.

The rich closing chapter of the feast at Coyote's Great House is an outstanding example of the kind of work we can present in *Case Studies in Archaeology*. It adds flesh to the already robust bones of archaeology. But it is not simply the resurrection of a prehistoric corpse, for Professor Hayden consistently demonstrates how Lillooet culture is an ongoing, vibrant continuum. His archaeological investigations have been enriched by information provided by living and recent native peoples and, in turn, he has contributed something to the understanding of a people's past. It would be a good thing if more archaeologists were as ethnographically sensitive as this author.

A spectacular site and setting, thorough presentation of technique, fascinating links between the past and present, and an intriguing theory of social change are wrapped in one neat package in this book. I am very pleased that it has found a home in the *Case Studies in Archaeology* series.

JEFFREY QUILTER

PREFACE

Understanding the nature of hunter–gatherers, and especially complex hunter–gatherers, is a quest that I have pursued over the last 20 years. Twelve of those years have been spent excavating and analyzing the materials from Keatley Creek, an unusually large winter housepit village on the edge of the British Columbia Plateau. This quest has been long and arduous and it has led to many unexpected areas, both geographical and intellectual. I have been constantly surprised by new facts, new relationships, new perceptions, new conclusions, and new questions. Some of these issues, such as the nature of elite power in transegalitarian societies, have made me return to old research areas, such as Mesoamerica, in order to clarify my perceptions of transegalitarian societies in general. Some of these issues, such as feasting, have led me to undertake new research projects, such as an ethnoarchaeological project focused on feasting among transegalitarian societies in Southeast Asia. The quest has never become dull or boring. If anything, it has been too interesting and too captivating. At times, it has been difficult to hold all the threads together in order to make a coherent tapestry of the past at Keatley Creek and to create coherent theoretical images of the past. However, the main themes have remained clear and resilient. I have found this venture to be genuinely exhilarating and a wonderful growing experience even if I have at times been exhausted by the endeavor.

As one of the largest housepit villages in western Canada, with some of the largest housepits on the Plateau, the site of Keatley Creek features very prominently in our understanding of complex hunters and gatherers. It is a site with many keys to understanding how our own form of hierarchical society with its elites, corporations, private ownership, and pronounced competitiveness emerged from much different egalitarian societies. Such transitions happened not only on the Plateau, but repeatedly in many different places throughout the world over the last 20,000 years or so. The transition from egalitarian types of societies to hierarchical ones is arguably the single most important cultural change that has occurred since the emergence of our ancestral hunting and gathering way of life some two million years earlier. Understanding how and why the transition to hierarchical society took place is one of the biggest challenges of contemporary archaeology. I have been fortunate to be able to pursue this quest in such a spectacular environment and with the assistance of many special people.

I am confident that as a result of the excavations at Keatley Creek, the new conceptual, methodological, and theoretical approaches that I and other analysts have developed will stimulate further advances in this exciting area of inquiry. However, many of the advances that we associate with this project have been fortuitous and serendipitous. I certainly did not foresee or plan for all of them. Many of the advances derived from interested students and analysts who became intrigued by the project and developed their own innovative ways of looking at the data. I have been constantly impressed by my very good fortune in having such dedicated and talented individuals involved in this project. It is they who have made it successful. Many of them are featured in the following chapters. There are many more individuals who have donated their time and efforts during the excavation and cataloging phases of the project. Although space is restricted, and I hope to acknowledge them all in the final site report, I would like to thank them all as a group here.

In this brief space, I would like to thank first and foremost those people that have generously permitted us to excavate on their legal and traditional lands: Mr. J. E. Termuende, of the Diamond S Ranch, and the Pavilion (Ts'qw'aylaxw) Indian Band. The Fountain (Xaxli'p) Indian Band has also provided substantial support. More than anyone else, Desmond Peters, Senior of the Pavilion Band, has been a mentor of our research in the area and has been invaluable in providing information on traditional culture. In the creation of this project, Dr. Arnoud Stryd was both an inspiration and a generous advisor. Morley Eldridge provided many seminal ideas and data as well. We have always been warmly welcomed by the people in the Lillooet region whether in meetings, at gatherings, on ranches, on reserves, in museums, or in stores; and we are grateful for their interest, their hospitality, and their friendship. Trevor Chandler, in particular, has been a constant supporter.

Many professionals have provided advice, comments, and suggestions during the course of this research and the writing of this book and I would particularly like to thank Roy Carlson, Phil Hobler, Jon Driver, R. G. Matson, Michael Blake, Mike Rousseau, Al McMillan, Rick Schulting, Ken Ames, Jim Chatters, T. Doug Price, Marvin Harris, Polly Wiessner, John Clark, Ernest Burch Jr., Jeffrey Quilter, and D'Ann Owens-Baird. Jim Spafford, Jaclynne Campbell, and Elizabeth Crowfoot spent many hours assembling the illustrations for which I am very grateful. Anita Mahoney navigated this manuscript through many incarnations, for which I am also very grateful. Jaclynne Campbell capably carried out the illustration program for the book.

Due to the vicissitudes of funding, there have been many agencies involved in the financing of this project. By far, the bulk of the funding has come from the Social Sciences and Humanities Research Council of Canada. Additional financing has been provided by the SSHRC Small Grants Committee at Simon Fraser University, the President's Research Committee at Simon Fraser University, the Simon Fraser University Special Research Projects Fund, and the British Columbia Heritage Trust. I would like to gratefully acknowledge the support of all of these agencies.

For instructors, students, or individuals who are interested in viewing the impressive geographical location of the Keatley Creek site, and in seeing some of the excavations and analyses in progress, a commercially available videotape titled *The Life and Death of the Classic Lillooet Culture,* can be procured from New Vision Media, Ltd., in Vancouver, British Columbia. This is a documentary program that has been widely broadcast on television in Canada. Information about the excavation at Keatley Creek may also be found on the World Wide Web at www.sfu.ca/archaeology/museum.

CONTENTS

Foreword   vi
Preface   ix

1   **COMPLEX HUNTER–GATHERERS
    AND THE KEATLEY CREEK SITE**   1
    The Setting   2
    Questions   5
    Trends in Cultural Evolution   7
    Complex Hunter–Gatherers   10

2   **THE COYOTE PEOPLE**   15
    Obtaining Food   18
    Social and Political Organization   22
    Recent Trends   23
    Summary   24

3   **PLANS AND PROCESSES**   27
    Choosing a Site and Planning Excavations   27
    Formation Processes   36
    Summary   42

4   **WHAT THE FEATURES REVEALED**   45
    Housepits   45
    Hearths   51
    Pit Features   53
    Postholes   56
    Roasting Pits   59
    Summary   60

5   **WHAT THE STONES HAD TO SAY**   61
    Tool Formation Processes   61
    Basic Distributions   63
    Activity Areas   69

Prestige Stones   72
Summary   75

6 WHAT THE PLANTS HAD TO SAY   77
Botanical Formation Processes   78
Distributions Across the Floor   78
Subsistence   82
Technology   83
Smoking   86
Summary   86

7 WHAT THE BONES HAD TO SAY   89
Formation Processes   89
Basic Distributions   93
The Mystery of the Dogs   97
Prestige Creatures   101
Bone Tools   103
Differences Between Housepits   103
Summary   106

8 BIG MAN, LITTLE MAN, BEGGAR MAN, FEAST   107
Mechanisms of Change and Hierarchies   110
Summary   118

9 TURNING OF THE SUN AT COYOTE'S GREAT HOUSE   121
Moon of the Turning Sun   121
Epilogue   128

References   131
Credits   137
Index   139

SERIES EDITOR

JEFFREY QUILTER

Washington, DC

THE PITHOUSES OF
KEATLEY CREEK

COMPLEX HUNTER–GATHERERS

OF THE NORTHWEST PLATEAU

CHAPTER I

Complex Hunter–Gatherers and the Keatley Creek Site

This book is about an unusual prehistoric community called Keatley Creek. The archaeological remains of this site are located in the Middle Fraser Canyon on the western edge of the Northwest Plateau of North America. This book is also about what archaeologists can discover of the inner workings of societies and cultures from the dust and fragments at ancient communities such as Keatley Creek. The results derived from these investigations can be used to understand the origin of the contemporary types of societies that we live in today with all their complexity, powerful corporations, and astonishing material miracles. Finally, this book explores the relationship between natural resources and the societies that use them.

To briefly take up this last point, we can observe that food and energy resources are necessary not only for the survival of our physical bodies, but also for the survival of cultures, cultural values, and ethnic identities. This is why land claims have been given such great importance by native and non-native groups alike: because these claims entail competing uses of resources for different cultural purposes. The urban and technological interface of industrial society has distanced most people from the nature of resource procurement and production in contemporary cultures. Nevertheless, the food and energy resources that modern societies depend upon have molded the nature of our societies, including our individual social relations, social institutions, cultural values, and our political institutions. The same has been true of all human societies in the past. By studying other societies, it is possible to learn a great deal about how resources affect our own behavior and our social or political institutions. This approach is often called "cultural ecology" (Steward, 1968). I will use the excavations at Keatley Creek as a prime example of how resources structured societies at a particularly important level of cultural evolution, the level represented by complex hunter–gatherers.

Complex hunter–gatherers exhibit the first private ownership of resources, the first significant social and economic inequality, and the first political concentration of power in cultural development. But before embarking on an exploration of the society and resources at Keatley Creek, it is necessary to set the stage for our study and provide some of the context that is essential to understand the remains of the Keatley Creek community.

THE SETTING

The Middle Fraser River Canyon in western Canada is a north–south stretch of 75 rough kilometers (km) in the 1,500 km course of the greatest remaining salmon river in the world (Figure 1.1). In this canyon area, a number of unusually large prehistoric housepit villages are located in the Lillooet region. The largest of them is located at Keatley Creek, about 25 km upstream from Lillooet, British Columbia (Figure 1.2). The region is known today for its spectacular topography and climatic extremes. In August 1994, during a week of 114 °F (42 °C) weather, native elder Maggie Mitchell recalled one winter when the temperature dropped to –60 °F (–52° C). In the neighboring Thompson Valley, another native elder told me he remembered one winter when the cattle froze standing up.

The original inhabitants of this region had to contend with these extreme temperatures as well as a precipitous topography. From its source in the Rocky Mountains, the Fraser River arcs westward across the northern reaches of the British Columbian Interior Plateau until it abuts against the high, snow and glacier-covered peaks of the Coast Range near Lillooet (Figure 1.1). It is here that it begins incising its way through the mountains to reach the coast, creating dizzying cliffs, narrow gorges, and majestic waterfalls. In 1808, Simon Fraser, the first Eurocanadian explorer in the region, experienced terror in crossing spindly, native scaffolds built across the sheer cliffs of the river at Hell's Gate. During his journey, he duly noted the many stories of Indians who fell to their deaths off cliff faces and trails. Today, the silt-laden Fraser River, named after Simon Fraser, continues to grind through bedrock sills along a major fault line that separates two great geological terranes. The river cuts through outwash gravels left by the last glaciers and it undercuts cliff faces at river bends, provoking, from time to time, catastrophic collapses of rock into the river far below.

For all the present-day majesty of the surrounding mountains and valleys, only 12,000 years ago, the entire earth's surface here was engulfed with ice to a depth of 2,000 meters (m). The ice in the upper zones flowed from east to west, at right angles to the deep rock-cut Fraser valley underneath that runs toward the south.

At the end of the Ice Age, 10,000 years ago, the melting of these thick masses of ice choked the Middle Fraser Valley with silt, sand, gravel, and boulders. This glacial detritus was deposited as flat outwash and till plains to depths of over 300 m with a thin veneer of fine silt dust (loess) covering the deposits like icing on a cake with thousands of layers. After the glaciers finished melting and filling the valleys with rock and pulverized sediments, the river began slicing through the loose gravels and sands leaving grass-covered terraces and abrupt canyon walls in a region now noted by geologists for its landslides and glacial features (Figures 1.3, 1.4).

When the original inhabitants of Keatley Creek came to live in this land, they wintered away from the river at the back edges of the terraces near the mountain bases. These locations provided some shelter from the harsh winter winds that funneled down the Fraser Valley, rushing far faster than freight trains toward the coast from their high pressure centers in the frozen Interior. These early campsite and village locations also provided wood from the mountain slopes, as well as water from creeks. In the springtime, the first inhabitants searched the surrounding hills for

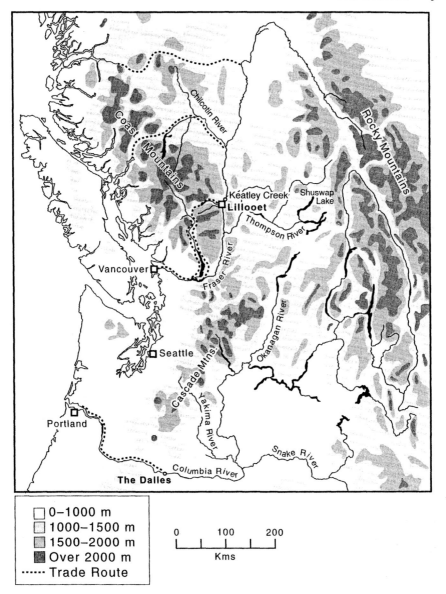

FIGURE 1.1. *Map of the Plateau geographical area of northwest North America. The British Columbian subarea of the Plateau extends from the northern reach of the Fraser River to the Canadian border with the United States, and from the Coast Mountains in the west to the Rocky Mountains in the east. The Columbian subarea of the Plateau extends from the Canadian border to the southern drainage of the Columbia and Snake Rivers, and from the Cascade Mountains in the west to the Rocky Mountains in the east. Note that there are only a few easily traveled major trade routes between the Coast and the Plateau.*

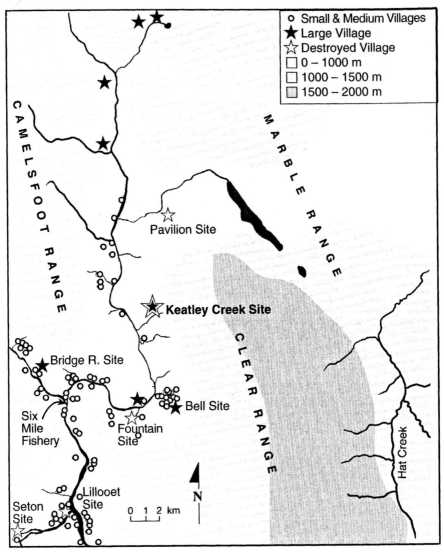

FIGURE I.2. *Map of the Lillooet region of British Columbia showing the distribution of prehistoric housepit sites and the location of Keatley Creek.*

signs of shoots or roots, or they scampered down the steep canyon walls hoping to catch a few of the early "spring" salmon. Later, in warmer weather, and again in the fall, they made the arduous trek to the high alpine meadows in the mountains behind their villages to hunt deer and collect rich, starchy alpine roots.

The village at Keatley Creek was located in a well-protected till depression and was sheltered from the severe winter winds. However, mere good shelter, wood, and water are insufficient to account for the presence of the large villages that developed in the Lillooet region—especially the unusually large villages. In addition to Keatley Creek, large villages were located at Bridge River, McKay Creek, and several

FIGURE 1.3. *Landslides have periodically sent massive amounts of rock plummeting into the Fraser River in the Middle Fraser Canyon as this relatively recent rock scar above the river indicates, as well as the older one to its left, now eroded into long skree slope. These slides are located only about 15 km downstream from the town of Lillooet.*

unnamed locations (see Figure 1.2). Others existed at Seton Lake, Texas Creek, Lochnore Creek, and probably at Pavilion Creek, Fountain Creek, and Lillooet itself, but these have been destroyed by modern roads, farming, mining, and land development. The very large prehistoric villages, ranging from 30 to 119 structures, occurred about every 5–10 km along the Fraser River in the Lillooet region. In addition to shelter, wood, and water, these large communities required great amounts of food to survive the winter. Carrying 40 kilogram (kg) packs of dried fish up precipitous heights from the river to the tops of terraces would have been arduous work, and it seems unlikely that people would have packed their winter supplies any farther than absolutely necessary, at least before horses were available. Thus, large villages were probably located relatively close to major sources of food such as salmon fishing locations.

QUESTIONS

But there are other unusual aspects to the large villages in the Lillooet region, and to the Keatley Creek village in particular. Notably, these villages contain unusually large housepit residential structures—semi-subterranean houses with timber roofs covered with earth and sod. In British Columbia, archaeologists refer to houses in use with the roofs still standing as *pithouses,* and houses with only the pit left as

FIGURE 1.4. *Once glaciers lay 2 km thick over these valleys. When they melted, 10,000 years ago, their debris filled the valleys with sand, gravel, and cobbles to the level represented by the terraces alongside the rivers today, such as Fountain Flats in this photograph. Later, the river began cutting through the debris left by glaciers resulting in the narrow gorges, such as this one that typifies much of the Middle Fraser Canyon.*

housepits. The villages contain a wide range of house sizes, from ones barely 5 m in diameter to houses almost 22 m in diameter. It is difficult to argue that the larger sizes were for purposes of warmth. If this was so, all houses should have been large, whereas few of them were. Architectural modeling shows that larger houses were less heat efficient than smaller ones. Thus, an important question concerns why some houses were so big. This is a problem that Lewis Henry Morgan (1881) raised over a century ago, but which has never been satisfactorily resolved. The tradition of building housepits at Keatley Creek, including the large varieties, goes back to the Shuswap Horizon (3500–2400 B.P.), persists through the Plateau Horizon (2400–1200 B.P.), and into the beginning of the Kamloops Horizon (1200–200 B.P.). It may have begun even earlier, but we have not been able to expose enough of the earliest deposits at the site to determine this. The earliest deposits date to the middle Prehistoric period, 7000–3500 B.P., and contain microblades, distinctive types of small, long, thin stone flakes that occur only during this time period. At this time, people were certainly camping at Keatley Creek and may have begun to build pithouses.

In addition to the basic questions concerning why the Lillooet villages (some might call them towns) were so large and why some of the residential structures within the villages were so big, there are many fascinating questions about Keatley Creek, some of which we will explore in the following chapters. These questions involve such topics as why dogs were domesticated in this region; just how complex the society at

Keatley Creek was; what the social and economic organization was like; how access to fish and other resources was regulated; the role that trade may have played in creating inequalities; and the importance that feasting served for creating hierarchies and inequality. But there is another, more mystifying question, namely, what happened to these large villages, for it appears that all the large villages were abruptly abandoned about 1,000 years ago. There is no evidence of warfare or mass burials. What happened to cause this sudden abandonment, and where did the inhabitants go?

The Lillooet region is an ideal context for dealing with many of the basic questions archaeologists would like to answer about the past social and economic organization of complex hunter–gatherers. The region is semiarid with only 200 mm of rain per year on average; sagebrush, grasses, and small prickly pear cacti occupy most of the terraces. This aridity creates excellent preservation conditions for plant, animal, and fish remains. Moreover, the occurrence of clearly distinguishable house remains, each associated with its own refuse midden, makes it easy to examine individual household behavior over time and to compare one household to another to understand economic or other differences. In addition, there is a rich and ongoing native tradition in the region which, at a general level, derives directly from the original occupants of the prehistoric communities that built housepits. The occurrence of all these elements (good preservation, distinct household remains, and pertinent ethnographic traditions) has enabled us to infer a remarkable amount of detail about the past life at Keatley Creek on the basis of the stones, bones, and botanical remains recovered. But where does this site and this culture fit in as far as the broad issues of archaeological models and debate are concerned?

TRENDS IN CULTURAL EVOLUTION

Over the last two million years, there have been fundamental changes in cultures everywhere in the world. Contrary to those who see only random patterns in evolution (e.g., Gould, 1987; Torrence, 1989), these changes exhibit strong patterning. One of the most striking characteristics of the patterned changes over the last 30,000 years involves the *independent* emergence of complex hunter–gatherers in numerous parts of the world from a substrate of generalized hunter–gatherers. This development first occurs during the Upper Paleolithic of Europe, but subsequently occurs in a more widespread fashion on *every* inhabited continent of the globe during the Epipaleolithic, Mesolithic, Archaic, or analogous Holocene periods. The most recurrent conditions associated with the rise of complex hunter–gatherers are Mesolithic-like food extraction and storage technologies combined with rich, natural food resources. I believe it is here where the search for causality should begin and where it is possible to clearly perceive one of the fundamental relationships of resources to culture.

Objective inspection of the archaeological record clearly shows that wherever food resource characteristics have been favorable, complexity and the total use of energy have increased in a fashion broadly consistent with the views of Steward (1955) and White (1957). This is not to say that cultures evolve in a strict unilinear fashion or that they never revert back to simpler organizational forms when environmental or other factors take a downturn. Cultures are, above all, interactive and situationally responsive. What the above and following observations do indicate is that there is a pattern to cultural developments that is comprehensible and this pattern does follow a type of basic evolutionary trajectory, or a limited number of them. In short, there appears to be more to understand about cultures than the relativistic relegation of cultural similarities and differences to haphazard bumberings.

In the panoply of prehistory, complex hunter–gatherers stand at a pivotal position in the evolution of cultures. But what are complex hunter–gatherers and how do they differ from other hunter–gatherers? Complex hunter–gatherers embody the first expression of significant social and economic inequality in the archaeological and cultural record. They exhibit the first widespread social and economic competitive behavior, the first significant private ownership of resources, and the first occurrence of large, relatively permanent settlements. Simple hunter–gatherers have none of these characteristics.

When we turn to the roster of major technological and social innovations, we find the first occurrences of metalworking, pottery, domestication of plants and animals, slavery, specialist production of art, and other prestigious technologies all occur in the context of complex hunter–gatherers. Moreover, these and other characteristics of nonegalitarian communities persist into horticultural communities with little basic alteration (Testart, 1982; Price & Brown, 1985, p. 17; Shnirelman, 1992). Therefore, understanding how complex hunter–gatherers were organized and why they emerged from more egalitarian, simple hunter–gatherers should reveal much about the origins of our own present-day society, as well as a great deal about how and why cultures change in general. It is not an exaggeration to say that the emergence of complex hunter–gatherers was the single most important development in cultural evolution since the first appearance of the genus *Homo* and the hunting–gathering lifestyle over two million years earlier. The emergence of complex hunter–gatherers was truly a watershed development in human history and it is intimately linked to the dramatic expansion of exploited food resources that characterized Mesolithic-type societies.

Here, I am using the term *Mesolithic* in its broad technological sense. Just as the term *Neolithic* refers to a type of economic and technological adaptation based on the production of food from domesticated plants and animals, so Mesolithic in a broad sense can refer to economic and technological adaptations based on the *systematic* (and often *intensive*) exploitation of fish, mollusks, seeds, nuts, and a broad spectrum of less important other plants and animals. Boiling and storage technologies are also usually part of this adaptation.

Another term requiring some comment is *complexity.* Societies can be complex in many different ways: in language, kinship, rituals, myths, art, economics, social institutions, politics, and other aspects. When archaeologists, such as Doug Price and James Brown (1985, p. 8) use the term *complex,* they are generally referring to aspects of these cultures that have the greatest effect on the material, or archaeological, remains left by societies. These aspects include social and economic inequalities (leading to the development of prestige items), centralization of political power (leading eventually to the construction of monumental buildings), and increased economic and political control (leading to larger, dominant settlements). Where resources support complex societies, the characteristics just mentioned usually give complex groups considerable advantages over simpler groups, especially in situations of competition and conflict. For all these advantages, complex societies also create less desirable outcomes, such as armed conflict and the impoverishment or disenfranchisment of some groups of people within their own communities. These features are much less developed among egalitarian hunter–gatherers but they characterize all complex societies, including the complex societies we live in today.

The following chapters are about one group of complex hunter–gatherers that lived on the North American Northwest Plateau from 3,500 to 1,000 years ago. The basic aim of the excavations I will describe is to understand the social and economic organization of one of the largest prehistoric communities of complex hunter–gatherers to have existed on the Northwest Plateau—the prehistoric Keatley Creek housepit village.

My primary interest in archaeology has always been to understand what life was like in the past, to discover not only the objects that people made and left behind, but also to learn why they made those objects, how people organized their lives, and how people related to their resources. I wanted to know why some groups, such as those at Keatley Creek, built unusually large houses, how they created and maintained inequalities between community members, why they developed prestige artifacts like nephrite adzes and copper pendants, and why they domesticated dogs. It is understanding the *why's* of behavior rather than the straightforward chronicling of past behavior that is of most interest to me. To understand the *why's* of behavior in past complex hunter–gatherers, it was obviously necessary to understand the constraints of the resources they had to deal with and how they used these resources to structure their society.

When I began this project, however, I was confronted with considerable skepticism from other archaeologists. In the 1960s, Processual archaeology planned to recover and explain all facets of prehistoric cultures, including their social, ideological, and economic organization. Processualists believed there were underlying, practical regularities in human behavior and choices which, given appropriate contexts, would make it possible to predict, or retrodict, at least the key developments and features of prehistoric communities. Such an ambitious interpretive program required valid theories that linked material remains to specific, identifiable types of behaviors and contexts. However, no such body of validated theories existed. There was even a protracted argument about whether hide-smoking smudge pits could be distinguished from similar pits with other functions. While considerable progress has been made in the intervening years, as we shall see, there still remain many unanswered questions concerning the precise behavior represented by archeological remains. Thus, there were few convincing or successful achievements in the realm of reconstructing or explaining past social organizations or other nontechnological aspects of culture. Post-Processualist archaeologists pointedly criticized Processualists for their failure to make progress in this domain. Even the high-profile, early research by Deetz, Longacre, and Hill was later argued to be flawed and misleading (Stanislawski, 1973, 1974, 1978; Plog, 1980). Other successful but more modest achievements (e.g., Whallon, 1968) were overlooked in the theoretical confrontations between Processual and post-Processual archaeologists.

In criticizing Processualists, the post-Processualists adopted many almost diametrically opposed positions. Post-Processualists argued there were no underlying principles of human behavior and that cultural values and beliefs played such important roles in determining behavior that the remains of each culture could be interpreted only in terms of themselves and their cultural "context." According to post-Processualists, individuals provided an internal dynamic element within cultures by pursuing their own interests and negotiating these interests with others. Since values, ideology, and cognitive cultural traditions played such central roles in the post-Processualist scheme of things, they were committed to recovering ideology through archaeological means. When combined with their emphasis on individuals, the post-Processualists were also committed to recovering past social organization. However, in contrast to Processualists, the post-Processualists rejected any notion that theories should be or could be tested. Post-Processualists even rejected the idea that an objective reality existed, not to mention the notion that we could ever know what was real in the past. With these assumptions, it is not surprising that most of the post-Processual attempts to recover past social organization and ideology were based on examples with historical, backup documents. There have been few, if any, successful or convincing analyses of purely prehistoric settlements.

Given the barrenness of these previous approaches, the archaeological climate did not inspire confidence that attempting to recover aspects of prehistoric social and economic organization from any site would be rewarding. Moreover, there were many regional archaeologists who doubted that undisturbed living floors of housepits could be identified or isolated given the many site formation processes that could mix sediments. These potentially confounding factors included the periodic reexcavation of housepits that could mix deposits from different periods, the filtering down of roof sediments with earlier artifacts onto living floors, mixing by burrowing animals and insects, and roof collapses, to name just a few.

Nevertheless, some previous excavators in the region, such as Arnoud Stryd (1973), felt that living floors could be recovered relatively intact, and that it would be possible to reconstruct at least the basic aspects of social and economic organization of Plateau housepit sites. Clutching to the encouragement provided by individuals like Arnoud Stryd and Morley Eldridge, I formulated some procedures I hoped would efficiently and effectively recover information on the prehistoric economic and social organization at the large, winter housepit villages in the Lillooet region. I feel that the results described in the following chapters will justify the initial faith and hope in the project's success. However, before turning to the archaeological remains of Keatley Creek, it will be useful to discuss the distinctive characteristics of complex hunter–gatherers in more detail and to alert readers to controversial issues associated with them.

COMPLEX HUNTER–GATHERERS

In an excellent summary article, Jeanne Arnold (1996) has defined complex hunter–gatherers as those groups exhibiting control over others' labor beyond immediate kinship relationships. This is primarily a statement about the development of political control, although it has many ramifications in terms of economic control, resources, establishing contractual agreements, feasting, mobility, and storage. I fundamentally agree with this definition. This is also a good definition for "transegalitarian" societies in general, a term which Clark and Blake (1989) have used to classify societies between egalitarian (generalized) hunter–gatherers and politically stratified chiefdoms. Clearly, all complex hunter–gatherers are transegalitarian societies, but so are most horticultural or tribal societies.

Although the difference between "generalized," or "simple" hunter–gatherers and complex hunter–gatherers has been noted for at least a century (Grosse, 1896; see also Birdsell, 1972; Wagner, 1960), it was largely unacknowledged or implicit in archaeological and ethnological studies until the 1970s (Price & Brown, 1985). Only at this time did researchers realize the profound ramifications that the distinction between generalized and complex hunter–gatherers might have for understanding cultural evolution. In fact, there is no evidence for the existence of complex hunter–gatherers until the Upper Paleolithic in Eurasia. During the Mesolithic (and the Archaic in North America) evidence of complex hunter–gatherers becomes more frequent, especially in resource rich areas, only to be transformed or supplanted by horticultural communities within a few thousand years.

Most complex hunter–gatherers occupy a narrow window of time in overall human and cultural evolution. Ethnographically, they persisted primarily in areas that were too cold or too dry, or otherwise too unproductive for horticulture—although, as in the Lillooet region, rich acquatic resources were generally available. Following are examples of complex groups that persisted until European contact: the Northwest Coast Indians; the Northwest Plateau groups; Northwest Alaskan Eskimos, the Koniag and the Aleuts; the Calusa in Florida; the California Chumash and neighboring groups; the Ainu; many Siberian fishers–hunters; southeast Australian groups; and the Tiwi in Australia. The best-known prehistoric representatives of complex hunter–gatherers include the Natufians, coastal or riverine Mesolithic groups in Europe and Siberia, the Jomon, many riverine or coastal Archaic groups in North America and South America, and the Upper Paleolithic groups that produced great art and jewelry.

In cultural ecological terms, one of the most consistent characteristics of all these groups is that they were able to exploit relatively abundant resources. Thus, they exhibit unusually high population densities for hunter–gatherers (from 0.1 to 10 people per square kilometer—Shnirelman, 1992, p. 188), and they were at least semi-sedentary. Many groups also relied heavily on stored foods in their more sedentary locations; however, not all did (e.g., the Calusa did not store much food), just as not all horticulturalists rely on stored foods. For example, some horticulturalists in New Guinea and Amazonia simply harvest their root crop staples as they are needed.

The issue of what specific environmental or technological conditions favor the development of complex hunter–gatherers is a contentious one that I shall return to in the concluding chapters. For the time being, it is sufficient to note that complex hunter–gatherers exhibit strong evolutionary patterning in terms of the environmental conditions, the associated technology, and the timing of their appearance. This patterning cannot be explained by appealing to changes in genetics, cognition, cultural norms, social relationships, or ideology. Appeals to these causes leave unanswered questions as to why such changes did not take place during the preceding 2 million years of prehistory, or why such changes should occur independently in so many areas of the world within the same 20,000-year period, and finally, why such changes should occur so consistently only in areas of rich resources. The emergence of complex hunter–gatherers under a limited range of environmental and technological conditions within a narrow time frame provides no clearer example of the fundamental role that both technology and resources play in cultural adaptations.

In terms of the cultural ecological distinction between generalized and complex hunter–gatherers, it is evident that the limited ability of generalized hunter–gatherers to extract resources from their environment has a great effect on their social and economic organization. These limitations may be due to the scarcity of resources in some environments such as deserts, or to the fact that the available technology is incapable of extracting, or storing, resources in any abundance. This seems to have been the case for most of the Paleolithic. As a result, generalized hunter–gatherers lived in small, highly mobile bands typically comprising only 25 to 50 individuals. Population densities were also low, from 0.01–0.1 people per square kilometer (Shnirelman, 1992, p. 188).

Due to fluctuations in resources and the potential for overexploiting important staples among generalized hunter–gatherers, sharing of food and other items was mandatory while any signs of selfishness constituted grounds for exclusion from the band. Similarly, any competition over economic resources or claims to exclusive use of these resources were prohibited by the majority of the band. All food resources, as well as food brought back to camp, were essentially communal property. Under these conditions any prestige objects that might be used for aggrandizing behavior were not only unacceptable, but they also made little sense in terms of self-interest. The extra effort needed to obtain them would not have been worth it since other members of the band could easily take, or "borrow," such objects for their own use. From an economic point of view, generalized hunter–gatherers are as close as human beings have ever been to a complete egalitarian, communal society. Each band was in essence one large family. Everything we know of the Lower and Middle Paleolithic conforms to this picture of generalized hunter–gatherers: low population densities; lack of middens due to the absence of recurring, intensive resource use; briefly occupied campsites; limited resource extraction potential; opportunistic hunting; limited or no food storage; and the lack of prestige objects.

The resources of complex hunter–gatherers were more abundant and usually more invulnerable to overexploitation due to high reproduction rates or the seasonal funneling of enormous numbers of animals from vast grazing regions into narrow migration routes. This resulted in higher human population densities in select areas as well as larger communities that were markedly more sedentary. Associated with these developments was an entire new suite of technological innovations that made it possible to obtain, process, and store fish, grass seeds, nuts, and migratory herd animals in great abundance. This represented a new systematic and intensive use of food resources. Travel to distant resources and transport of bulk foods was probably made possible by boats, sleds, or travois. Under these conditions, changes in social and economic relations were profound.

For instance, private ownership of some important food resources developed, as well as private ownership of the means of obtaining food (such as Chumash boats, and Northwest nets, weirs, fishing platforms, and deer fences). Moreover, progressively more resources became owned as complexity increased.

Ownership of gathered, stored foods probably resulted initially from two factors. First, extra work was required to prepare foods for storage and to create good storage facilities. This extra effort probably motivated people to view the products as their own. Second, only where resources were temporarily overabundant did it make sense to put large quantities aside for storage. Given great abundances, each family should have been able to obtain their own shares of food unless they were lazy. Therefore, in places like the Northwest Plateau, each family owned their own stored foods. This is related to another characteristic of complex hunter–gatherers.

As Testart (1982, p. 526) has observed, in general, the storage of large amounts of food leads to reduced sharing. This occurs in part because sharing was a means of reducing the risk of future food shortages, and storage provided an alternate means of reducing the risk of food shortages. The lessened emphasis on sharing probably also resulted from the same factors that led to private ownership, the abundance of resources and the increased effort required to store them. Whatever the ultimate cause, in contrast to the liberal, even compulsory, sharing of food by generalized hunter–gatherers, people who asked for food under normal conditions in complex hunter–gatherer communities, such as those of the Northwest Plateau, were denigrated as "lazy moochers." Although if food shortages were widespread those who had surpluses were expected to help those without.

Competition based on the economic production of surpluses also emerged between families, groups, and communities, with the result that some groups became rich while others became poor. Thus, social and economic hierarchies emerged, together with prestige technologies to display the greater status of wealthy and powerful individuals. These distinctions were often manifested in burial rites and grave goods, as well as extensive regional trade networks for prestige goods. Ethnographically, slavery appeared among the more complex hunter–gatherers probably as another means of displaying power and success. Why these hierarchies should have emerged under conditions of abundant resources invulnerable to overexploitation is a topic that will be addressed in chapter 8.

This is a rough composite portrait of complex hunter–gatherers drawn from cross-cultural ethnographies. Do the archaeological remains of complex hunter–gatherers support such a portrait in this basic form, and if so, what details are possible to establish from the archaeological record of sites like Keatley Creek? These are the topics of the following chapters. Dealing with such topics is our ultimate goal, but before answering these questions, it is necessary to address two other areas for our investigation to proceed on a firm footing. First, it will be useful to become familiar with the native cultures of the area—the descendants of the prehistoric residents of Keatley Creek. Second, it is necessary to determine what kinds of deposits are actually present at Keatley Creek and to what extent they have been disturbed or modified. In brief, we must identify the site formation processes that created the soils and the cultural debris at the site.

CHAPTER 2
The Coyote People

Because native life and culture is so important to understanding archaeological remains in North America, we shall take a brief look at what traditional life was like in the Lillooet region before examining the archaeological remains from Keatley Creek in detail. There are three native linguistic groups that converge on the site catchment area of Keatley Creek (Figure 2.1). This is the area around the site that would have been regularly used for obtaining food resources. These linguistic groups are the Stl'atl'imx (or St'at'imc; pronounced Shtla-tlye-mkh, also known as the Fraser River Lillooet Indians), the Nlaka7pamux (pronounced N-le-ka'-p-mkh, also known as the Upper Thompson Indians), and the Secwepemc (pronounced Sha-khwep-makh, also known as the Shuswap Indians).[1] All three languages are members of the Interior Salish language family, and all three claim to be descended from a coyote ancestor who is the most prominent figure in their oral traditions (Teit, 1917, p. 12). All three groups also have similar material culture. Therefore, archaeologists have not been able to distinguish these groups from each other prehistorically, and we cannot say for certain which of the three languages was spoken by the prehistoric residents of Keatley Creek. However, because there is an unbroken cultural tradition throughout the Salish-speaking part of the Plateau, from middle Prehistoric times (ca. 7000 B.P.) until contact with Eurocanadians in the 1800s, it seems almost certain that the residents of Keatley Creek spoke one of the Interior Salish languages.

Because of the strong cultural continuity in the area (especially from about 3500 B.P. onward, when semisubterranean housepits and a strong reliance on salmon first became widespread), observations on traditional native life should provide

---

[1] Henry Davis, who works with Lillooet language, has provided the following pronunciation guide for these terms:

St'at'imc: The first sound is (approximately) as in English "*ship.*" The second is produced by putting the tongue in position for a dental t, then, producing an ejective by trapping air between the tongue and glottis, raising the glottis, then releasing the t into a lateral fricative, which is like a "whispered" l. The third sound is something between the vowel in "cat" and "bet," the fourth is a glottalized (creaky) "y," then a plain old m and then a sound halfway between ch in German "ich" and ch in Scottish "loch."

Nlaka7pamux: N is a syllable on its own. The l is a whispered l (lateral fricative) like Llewellyn in Welsh; "a" is like "e" in bed; k is nonaspirated as in skin, not kin. The 7 is a glottal stop; the middle sound in uh(7)oh; p as above; the third a is not pronounced; mux as in mc above (just different orthographic representation).

Secwepemc: First sound is like English "s" (approximately). Second is a schwa (like the a in "about." Third, (cw) round the lips as you produce the "c" sound described in St'at'imc above. Fourth, "e" as in "bed." Next, nonaspirated "p" as in "spit" (not "pit"). Then another schwa, and last two as above.

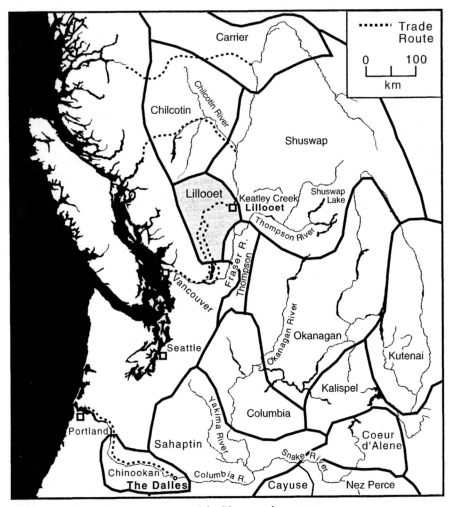

FIGURE 2.1. *Map of language groups of the Plateau culture area.*

many insights into past cultures of the region. The ethnographic observations made around 1900 have greatly aided us in understanding the functions of tools such as bark peelers, digging-stick handles, hide scrapers, the use of plants, and a host of other details that would otherwise remain as unexplained curiosities. However, ethnographic observations must always be used cautiously since tool uses, behaviors, and other conditions sometimes change from prehistoric to historic periods. I have distinguished a number of types of ethnographic analogies that differ in terms of their reliability and applicability (Hayden, 1993, p. 127). The type of ethnographic analogy that I use most at Keatley Creek is referred to as "synthetic cultural analogy" since it is a synthesis of several distinct, but closely related groups (the Stl'atl'imux, the Nlaka7pmux, and the Secwepemc). It has a high reliability value. For instance, it is almost certain that the objects we recovered resembling the illustrations of historic digging-stick handles and bark peelers were actually used for these purposes (Figure 2.2). On the other hand, synthetic culture analogies are

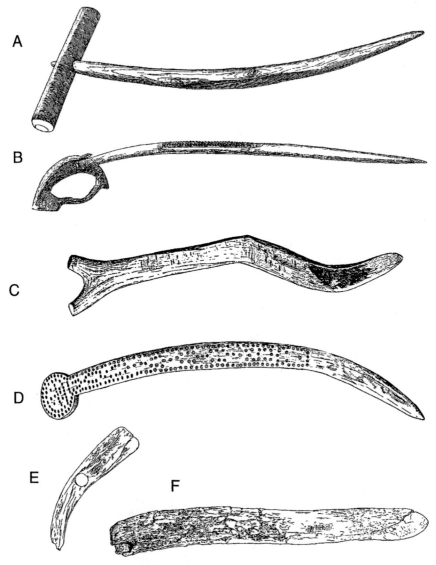

FIGURE 2.2. *Illustrations of digging-stick handles (A, B) and bark peelers (C, D) that James Teit recorded in use among Interior Salish groups in the 19th century are very similar to archaelogical examples of digging-stick handles (E) and bark peelers (F) recovered at Keatley Creek from a thousand years earlier. Ethnographic analogy is very useful in determining the functions of archaeological items in such cases.*

limited in their applicability to the groups from which they are derived, that is, to the Interior Salish and possibly other Plateau groups. This is still a relatively large geographical area for the use of these analogies.

From 1898 to 1912, James Teit described in remarkable detail the traditional life of all three of the Interior Salish groups. Teit had married a Nlaka7pmux woman and learned much of the language. He had an abiding interest in native cultures, and fortunately was also able to record much of these details in writing with some help from Franz Boas. The following descriptions are largely based on Teit's accounts, although many traditional activities such as salmon fishing continue to play an important role in people's lives right up to the present. It has therefore been possible to obtain more details about important aspects of traditional lifestyles as recently as this decade (see Hayden, 1992).

OBTAINING FOOD

Ethnographically, the most important resource throughout the region was salmon. And the most productive fishery along the Interior Fraser River was located about 10 km upstream from the modern town of Lillooet at a place called the Six Mile Fishery, or the "Fountain"—referring to the cascade in the Fraser River at that location (see Figures 1.2, 2.3). Many other rich fisheries extended up and downstream from that point. The most productive fishing locations were at points where rocks jutted into the river, or where the river was restricted. The farther one could reach with a net, the more and the larger salmon it was possible to obtain. Therefore, people often built platforms out into the water to catch the most and the best salmon (Figure 2.4). These fishing sites and platforms were owned by families, although there were other fishing sites open to the public.

FIGURE 2.3. *An aerial view of "The Fountain," today known as the Six Mile Rapids and Fishery. The narrow constriction of the river is difficult for salmon to ascend, so they gather in pools behind the rock jetties below the rapids where they are caught by fishermen. Traditionally, each of these jetties was owned and had a platform erected to assist in catching fish. Today, the structures for drying fish can be seen on the rock terraces above the river.*

FIGURE 2.4. *Traditional fishing platforms such as these were constructed by Indians on the Plateau to reach the larger and more numerous salmon that swam in deeper waters. These platforms were in use near The Dalles on the Columbia River, but similar ones were also used along the Fraser River.*

Fishing in this fashion was frequently dangerous, especially when several large salmon weighing up to 30 or 40 kg each struck the large, traditional hoop nets. Fishermen took their lives into their hands when they stood on narrow ledges or springy platforms to catch salmon. Having a rope tied around the waist and secured to something on land saved many fishermen from plunging into the roiling currents of the Fraser River, a river that sucked people under the water and sometimes did not return them to the surface for days, many kilometers downstream. At the peaks of the salmon runs, fishermen could catch hundreds of salmon in a hour, but they generally became fatigued after only a half an hour of this intensive activity.

It was the women's work to butcher and dry the salmon, and this took more time than the catching of salmon. On average, a woman could process about 50 to 60 salmon per day, hanging them to dry in the hot, late summer winds of the Fraser Canyon for about three to four days. Thus, for a household to have large quantities of dried salmon for the winter and for trade, they needed access to the better fishing locations with platforms, and also enough women to help process all the fish that were caught. It is probable that the importance of women for producing dried salmon helped establish the practice of wealthy men taking many wives (historically, up to 10 wives). The fishing sites, like other important prerogatives, were inherited in the male line. In most Interior Salish groups, women's status was lower than men's although among the Stl'atl'imx and the rich Canyon Shuswap, their status seems to have been well above their Salish sisters elsewhere on the Plateau. This is consistent with trends elsewhere in the world where richer transegalitarian societies use marriage exchanges to invest and increase wealth, thereby placing women in critical brokering positions (Hayden, 1995).

In the Lillooet region, each family required hundreds of dried salmon to last out the winter in their pithouses. There were substantial variations in catches from year to year, with spectacularly large runs every fourth year, as well as occasional years of low water levels and almost no salmon. Being able to store salmon from one year to the next was very important. After the salmon runs had subsided in early fall, most families stored their dried salmon on roofed, elevated platforms by the river. They also carried a substantial portion up the steep canyon slopes to their winter village where it was either stored in pits or on platforms. After storing dried salmon at their village locations in the fall, the families continued to trek up the mountain slopes until they reached the high alpine areas where the deer had congregated (Figure 2.5). By September to October, the deer had built up their fat stores and their fur was in prime condition for the coming winter. Fat was especially important for people in this area to provide enough calories to keep warm; carbohydrates were relatively rare in the diets of Interior peoples. Fat is constantly mentioned and emphasized in the myths of the Interior Salish people recorded by James Teit.

In the mountains, perhaps some of the domesticated native dogs helped run down the deer. When not collecting whitebark pine nuts, the women defleshed the skins of the killed deer. Skins that they did not have time to work into buckskin by the arduous, traditional tanning techniques were dried and brought back to the winter village to be worked on during the winter. Because deer were not very plentiful and because of the great labor required to produce buckskin, tanned skins and especially buckskin clothes were greatly valued. Not everyone had them. Poor people wore clothes of sagebrush bark. Deer meat, too, was highly valued and was dried in the mountains and taken back to the winter village for use in feasts.

When the days turned too cold to stay in the alpine areas, when the snows began to accumulate, families returned to their winter villages where they had stored dried foods for the winter: salmon, deer meat, fat, berries, and some roots gathered in the spring. In the pithouses, they worked on repairing tools, fishing nets, making skin clothes, and other crafts. When the weather was not too cold they went hunting (for the deer were forced down to lower altitudes by deep snow) and some people went ice fishing. They feasted and danced, and between events, they snuggled and slept, almost as though they were hibernating.

By March, stored supplies generally ran low, either due to feasting or due to poor harvests. People were anxious to get out of their winter places and went in search of early berry shoots, onions, balsam root, cow-parsnip, fireweed, lodgepole pine cambium, or other plants. Some people went down to the river to fish for the "spring" or chinook, salmon that returned in sparse numbers. When the snows had cleared from the intermediate grasslands, people went to the mountains to collect berries, various lily roots, and "mountain potatoes" (*Claytonia lanceolata,* also known as "spring beauty") as well as to hunt. Women dried many of these plants and brought back as much as they could carry down the mountain to their winter village.

As the weather warmed the alpine areas, many people continued their migration into these higher areas to harvest the lily roots, berries, and mountain potato

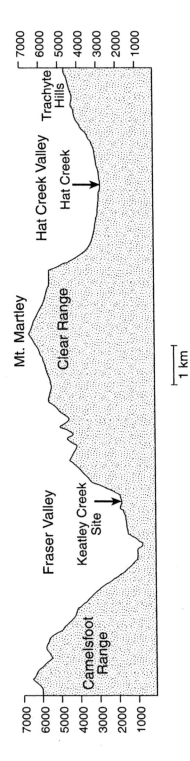

FIGURE 2.5. A cross section of the topography from the Camelsfoot Mountains, through Keatley Creek, to the alpine peaks of the Clear Range, and through the Hat Creek Valley. The prehistoric occupants of Keatley Creek made the arduous trek to the alpine areas and Hat Creek to collect plant foods and to hunt, probably twice a year just as their historic descendants did. (Vertical scale is exaggerated.)

roots, and they undoubtedly hunted along the way. Other families went to the mountain lakes to fish for trout. By the time they brought dried mountain plant foods back to the winter villages for storage in June or July, Saskatoon or service berries were ready for harvesting at lower elevations, and people gathered many bark buckets of the sweetest berries for storage. By the end of July, the salmon were running and families moved down to the rivers once again to begin fishing for the winter.

SOCIAL AND POLITICAL ORGANIZATION

Social and political complexity varied considerably between peoples of the Interior Plateau. Those areas with the most productive fishing locations such as the Lillooet communities, the Canyon Shuswap, and farther south, the Wishram and Wasco communities at The Dalles on the Columbia River, all had quite complex social and political organizations. The people of these regions controlled major trade routes to the coast as well, and they must have enhanced their surplus-based trading profits due to this fact. The elites in some of these areas tried to restrict trade to themselves. They controlled bridges and trade routes and charged fees for using them (Ferguson, 1984, pp. 286–287, 304, 314; Teit, 1909, pp. 535, 541, 576, 583). At The Dalles they even charged Lewis and Clark a fee for transiting their territory.

Chieftainship was hereditary, slavery and trade were important, and there were many kinds of feasts including potlatches, although these may not have been as spectacular as those on the coast during the years the fur trade was booming. Ownership of facilities that required substantial labor to construct was inherited through males and stayed within families. These facilities included deer fences, salmon platforms, and fishing rocks. House structures were inherited through women. Houses and owned resource locations were often marked with carved or painted crests (totemic animals) indicating their owners. Trade, exchange, and the wealth that resulted from them seem to have been more important than warfare, and these wealthy, complex groups were noted for their non-warlike attitudes. Wealth consisted of owned fishing locations, of dentalium and other shells traded from the coast, of buckskin clothes, furs and warm bedding, of wives, of stores of meat and fat, of eagle feathers and other bird plumage, of slaves, canoes, and of nephrite adzes. The wealthy families shared with the poor when the spectre of starvation haunted the poorer families, but the rich complained about the lazy moochers in their communities. When men of wealth died, their dogs and slaves were reported to have been sometimes killed at the interrment and the sacrificed dogs suspended from poles (Teit, 1906, pp. 269–270; 1909, p. 593). With such inequalities in wealth and power, with slave and hereditary elite classes, and with ownership of resources and the means of production, these were clearly complex hunter–gatherers.

James Teit (1909, p. 576) described the following:

> The Fraser River bands were divided into three classes,—noblemen, common people, and slaves. The first class were called "chiefs," and constituted . . . nearly *one-half to over two-thirds of the whole population* [italics added]. The nobles had special priviledges, and generally married within their class. Nobility was hereditary, and seems to have descended in both the male and the female line. Women of this class

appear to have been on an equality with the men. . . . The crest of the (noble) group was carved and painted on the top of the ladder of the underground house, the ladder frequently being made very long for this purpose . . . representations of the crest were also erected at the main fishing-places . . . and also at their graves.

Teit (1906, p. 258) also mentions potlatches:

> Potlatches were given by one individual to another or by the chief of one clan to another . . . the chief represented his clan, and the potlatch was equivalent to one given by all the members of one clan to all the members of another. Some of these potlatches were great affairs; and *clans tried to outdo one another by the quantity and value of their presents, thus showing to all the country that they were most powerful, wealthy, and energetic.* . . . In most cases the *guests were expected at some future day to return presents equal in value to those given to them, or even of greater worth* [italics added].

Later, Melena Nastich (1954, pp. 23–25, 83) obtained the following information:

> Wealthy households were large, consisting not only of the offspring of polygynous marriages, but of a number of slaves and of a fringe of poor relatives . . . some such households numbered up to thirty people. *Each nuclear family of spouses and their offspring occupied its own living space, possessed its own cooking rocks* [italics added], baskets, blankets, and eating utensils, but functioned in close harmony with other members in social and economic pursuits. . . . High social standing . . . was the result of accumulated wealth and recognized achievement. High standing families carefully avoided marriage with low status families for fear of jeopardizing the wealth and social status of the household.

Elsewhere on the Plateau, where salmon and other resources were less plentiful, leadership was not determined as much by inheritance as by ability. Slaves were less important and ownership of resource locations was less prevalent. Many of these groups are noted for their egalitarian ethic, which Verne Ray and others assumed was characteristic of all Plateau groups. In reality this represented only one end of the full Plateau spectrum.

Groups with less abundant and less reliable resources were more noted for their warlike nature and regularly raided those groups with a stockpiled surplus of dried fish and meat. Occasionally there were great wars. Women's status in these leaner and meaner groups was generally not very high. It is less clear that the communities at this end of the spectrum represented very complex hunter–gatherers.

RECENT TRENDS

Shortly after the gold rush that seriously affected Lillooet and many other Interior communities in 1858, the British Columbia government acted to preempt most of the land claimed by natives in the Interior, including most of their resources. The government left only what can be called "postage stamp" reserves, although they included many of the important fishing locations. These events are engagingly chronicled by Joanne Drake-Terry (1989). With the introduction of highly efficient, highly desirable (and in the case of firearms, even necessary items for self-protection) industrial goods, coupled with the restriction and devaluation of native resources, native communities found themselves in impoverished economic situations.

The reduced relative value of their resources and the physical diminishment of those resources due to logging, placer mining, damming, farming, ranching, and other industrial activities all meant that native Indians had to contend with more limited and increasingly scarce resources. These are the same resource conditions that had made generalized hunter–gatherer values and social institutions so adaptive. And like generalized hunter–gatherers, the pressures on the colonized Interior Indians to become more egalitarian and to share their limited resources within communities became overpowering. Owned deer fences were abandoned, deer meat became less valuable, the European potato was called "chief," people no longer recognized ownership of fishing rocks, and hereditary leadership was abandoned. Thus, the resources that people had to depend upon strongly influenced the nature of their social and political organizations. In this case, diminished value and availability of resources led to an abandonment of resource ownership and hereditary privileges. In recent years, there has been a trend to view the current egalitarian ethics of the modern communities as typical of all past Interior cultures. But any dispassionate reading of the early ethnographies clearly indicates this was not so (see Scheffel, 1994, and comparable observations on the coast by Donald, 1985, p. 241).

Other changes have also taken place. During the Great Depression and Second World War, many families relied to a great extent on traditional foods. Much traditional subsistence knowledge was retained during these years. With increasing wage labor opportunities from the 1950s to the present, many of the labor intensive and low-yielding subsistence activities have been abandoned. Today, almost no one goes to the mountains to collect lily roots or other food plants. On the other hand, hunting is still popular, as is fishing, although the techniques have been modernized and chinook salmon are no longer valued as the prime salmon species. Now sockeye salmon are more highly valued, I suspect because the flesh is less oily and more easily dried. Fish with high oil content would have been valuable under traditional conditions for the same reasons that fat was highly valued, that is, to provide enough calories for adequate body heat in the cold winters. Preservation techniques have also changed, with most dried fish today also being put into freezers.

Although much oral heritage and knowledge has been lost in the last four decades, there is still a strong cultural identity on the part of members of Interior Salish bands and many people continue to engage in productive, traditional subsistence activities.

SUMMARY

Ethnographic observations help not only to identify the use of unusual types of tools, but in regions like the Plateau, this information can also establish the range of social and political organizations that archaeologists may encounter in investigating past cultures. In the case of the Interior Salish, there is a surprisingly broad range of sociopolitical organizations. These extend from nearly egalitarian communities to communities that appear to be quite stratified both economically and socially, but not politically. Economic stratification occurs when some individuals or families own resources or the means of production and others do not. Social stratification occurs when there are separate, hierarchical social classes, such as nobles and slaves. Political stratification occurs when one community controls the independence of other communities in a hierarchical fashion. Transegalitarian societies are frequently economically and socially stratified, but are not politically stratified. Observations on the regional range of cultural organization help to focus archaeologists' attention on key questions in their research, such as how complex the prehistoric community at Keatley Creek was and what kinds of evidence are associated with different levels of complexity.

From the preceding discussion, it appears that highly productive salmon fishing locations, the occurrence of wealth items, reduced warfare, and rich burials are some of the phenomena one should expect with more complex communities of hunter–gatherers. This use of ethnographic observations is referred to as using "analogy from principle" because it is based on the identification of causal principles. In this case, a cultural materialist perspective leads us to expect that the effective harvesting and storage of abundant salmon resources generated wealth and inequalities. Lavish displays of wealth in burials and houses characterize some families. Such displays of success might be especially important where succession to power and resources is unstable and competitive (Randsborg, 1982, p. 135; Cannon, 1989). Surplus wealth should also enhance the importance of exchange resulting in a reduction of warfare. Such principles again demonstrate how resource characteristics affect social complexity. When well substantiated and documented, these types of analogies are among the most powerful that archaeologists can use. They are broadly applicable and they are generally quite reliable. Although, as with the laws of physics, one must always be aware that other factors can change expected outcomes, just as hot air balloons seem to contravene the law of gravity. However, like all levels of analogy that generate new insights, specific interpretations must always be tested with archaeological data. No analogy should be accepted as valid unless it also conforms with the archaeological evidence.

Ethnographic observations on the changes that have taken place from traditional precontact times to historic and present times also reveal how changes in the nature of resources, technology, and economy can lead to profound changes in social relationships, private ownership, political institutions, and values. As the nature of resources changes, people's perceptions also change regarding social relationships, claims to resources, degrees of sharing, and political relationships that are in their best interest. This is as true today as it was 2,000 or 200,000 years ago.

CHAPTER 3
Plans and Processes

CHOOSING A SITE AND PLANNING EXCAVATIONS

With the goal of investigating prehistoric social and economic organization of complex hunter–gatherers firmly in mind, and having heard stories of unusually large dwellings in the Interior Plateau of British Columbia, my students and I began a thorough search of the recorded housepit village sites of British Columbia to find the largest structures. On the basis of previous work on Iroquoian longhouses (Hayden, 1977; Hayden & Cannon, 1982), I reasoned that large houses would constitute a distinctive type of social and economic organization. I referred to large, multifamily houses as *residential corporate groups*. It seemed that the chances of recovering social organization would be best if we concentrated on such corporate structures. If I was right, then the economic and social characteristics of large multifamily dwellings should be substantially different from small houses and should provide clues to the reasons for the formation of the large dwellings.

The archaeological site at Keatley Creek (Figures 3.1, 3.2) not only had the largest houses recorded for the Interior of British Columbia, but also had the highest

FIGURE 3.1. *A general view of the core of the Keatley Creek site. The actual creek is in the ravine to the left.*

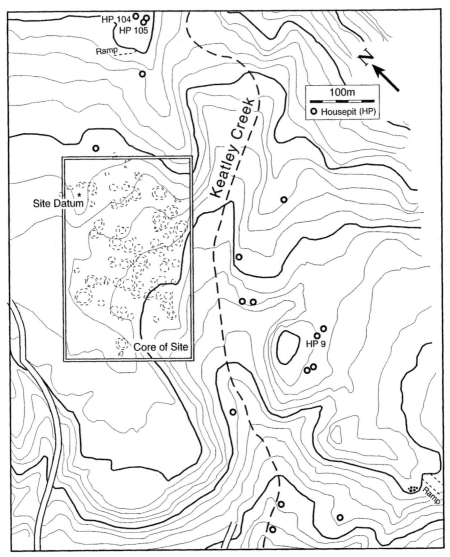

FIGURE 3.2. *A contour map of the full site area at Keatley Creek. The core area covers about 5 ha, while isolated housepits and cachepits in outlying areas of the site cover at least another 8 ha. Several structures and small features also occur along the creek about 70 m upstream from the top of the map. Contour interval = 5 m.*

number of houses recorded for any site. I therefore decided to concentrate excavations at Keatley Creek, and the Fraser River Investigations of Corporate Group Archaeology project was born with financial assistance from the Canadian Social Sciences and Humanities Research Council.

The second step was to determine which houses at Keatley Creek to excavate. As is evident from the site map (Figure 3.3), there are only five or six very large housepits out of the 120 structures at the site. Thus, we placed narrow (50 cm wide) test trenches from the edge to the center of all the large housepits, as well as in a number

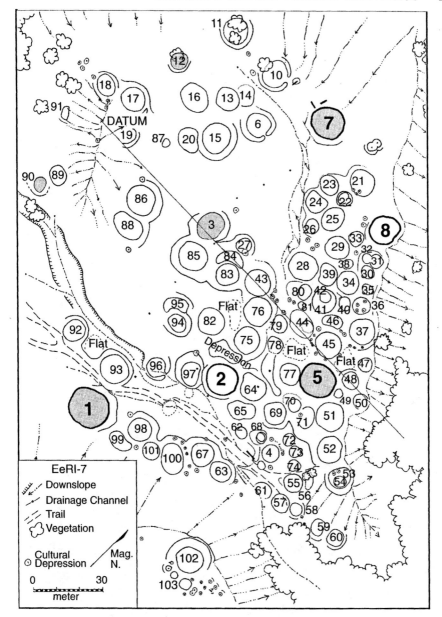

FIGURE 3.3. *Map of the core of the Keatley Creek site with housepit numbers indicated. Excavated housepits mentioned in the text are highlighted in gray, and the five largest housepits are designated in bolder numbers.*

of medium and small housepits. These houses were chosen on a judgmental basis to emphasize the perimeters of the site where we assumed there would be less disturbance from rebuilding. The sampling design may not have been statistically sophisticated; however, there was really nothing warranting a random sample in this case. We excluded all structures that had been cut into by later building activity, as well as the vast majority of structures that were crowded into the center of the site, and structures that had been badly disturbed by pothunters. Ultimately, we tested 24 of the structures at the site, or about 20% of the total.

This testing phase of the structures provided a number of extremely valuable observations about the site. First, it became clear that the vast majority of deposits at the site could be divided into several basic types. Following are the most important types:

1. *Sterile till.* These sediments were composed of yellowish sands, silts, and gravels that glaciers had ground up and left as mixed homogeneous deposits on the bottoms and sides of valleys after the glaciers melted.

2. *Floor deposits* in houses. These deposits sometimes had slightly less gravel, were generally dark gray, but could vary in color and texture depending on the length of occupation and other factors. (Figure 3.4).

3. *Roof deposits.* These sediments had very high gravel, silt, and sand contents similar to the till parent material. They were typically dark gray and homogenous.

4. *Rim deposits.* These deposits varied dramatically from lenses consisting almost completely of dry organic material that literally floated in water, to roof-like lenses, to lenses that were essentially the same as the sterile underlying till.

A second result of our housepit testing program revealed that the larger structures and most medium-sized structures had thick midden deposits forming the "rim" around the housepit depressions (Figure 3.5). Typically, the bottom of these

FIGURE 3.4. *The distinctive color differences that sometimes showed up between the roof and floor deposits is clearly evident in this excavation unit while in others, the occurrence of burned beams clearly demarcated the roof sediments from the floor sediments.*

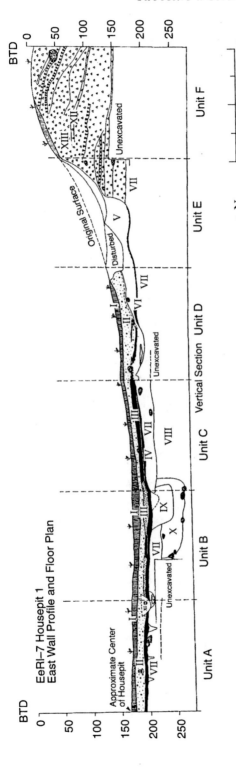

FIGURE 3.5. *Cross section of a typical large housepit test trench extending from the center of the house (at left) to the top of the rim midden that encircles the house (at right). Note in particular the large storage pit under the floor and the clearly stratified nature of the rim deposits. Floor deposits are solid black. The rim strata maintain approximately the same dip, or angle, from the middle of the rim to its top, indicating that the overall house size had probably not changed significantly during this period and perhaps even earlier.*

rim deposits was stratified and contained only Shuswap projectile point types (Figure 3.6), dating to 2400–3500 B.P. The middle zones of the rim middens were also stratified and contained primarily Plateau projectile point types dating to 1,200–2,400 years ago; while the uppermost level was not stratified, but mixed, resembling the roof deposits, and contained a mixture of Plateau and Kamloops points, the latter dating from 1200–200 B.P. These results indicated that the large- and medium-sized houses were occupied from the initial housebuilding period of the site and continued to be occupied at least intermittently to the end of the site's history about 1,000 years ago. The occupation of large houses in large winter sites over this entire period is what I refer to as the classic Lillooet culture. If you examine Figure 3.5 carefully, you will note the layers throughout most of the rim's depth are intact; they have not been mixed in a fashion that happens when rototillers or people dig up earth. Thus, these deposits have not been significantly disturbed from the time they were originally deposited. Moreover, the angle or dip of the lenses within the rims do not change in their basic orientation. This constitutes an important bit of information. It shows that the large and medium houses with these deep, intact, rim deposits stayed about the same size from when they were originally built during Shuswap horizon times, until the time the site was abandoned.

A third important result of the housepit testing program revealed that small housepits, almost without exception, had no organic buildup of midden material in their rims. There was not any significant accumulation of worn-out stone tools or debris in these rims as there was with the larger housepits. Nor were the rims or roof deposits of the small housepits deeply discolored from charcoal or other organic matter. In short, all indications show that the smaller housepits were used only for comparatively brief periods of time, perhaps a few years or a generation or two, but certainly not the hundreds and thousands of years represented by the larger structures.

A fourth important result of the housepit testing program was the establishment of a clear chronology for the site, beginning with diagnostic bladelet deposits from the middle Prehistoric period (3500–7000 B.P.) found underneath the rim deposits of houses, through the Shuswap, Plateau, and Kamloops horizons. We were able to confirm that the changes in styles of projectile points found at Keatley Creek corresponded to changes in point styles during each of the cultural horizons that typified the Interior Plateau as a whole (see Figure 3.6; Richards & Rousseau, 1987; Stryd & Rousseau, 1995). These changes in projectile point style are much like the changes in style over time of automobiles, or Coke bottles, or telephones, with which we are all familiar.

A fifth important result from the housepit testing program, and one of the main objectives of the testing program, was that we were able to identify those housepits that had the clearest distinctions between the various types of deposits. I was particularly interested in locating structures where the floor deposits could be easily seen. It was from these living floors that we had the best chance for recovering details of how the individuals within the houses organized their social and economic activities and how families differed in terms of activities, wealth, or other aspects. To be sure, it was possible to make coarse observations on the overall social and economic differences between houses as entire entities, but if it were possible to study the details of the internal organization of each house, this would provide far greater information on the social and economic life of the prehistoric inhabitants of Keatley Creek. When

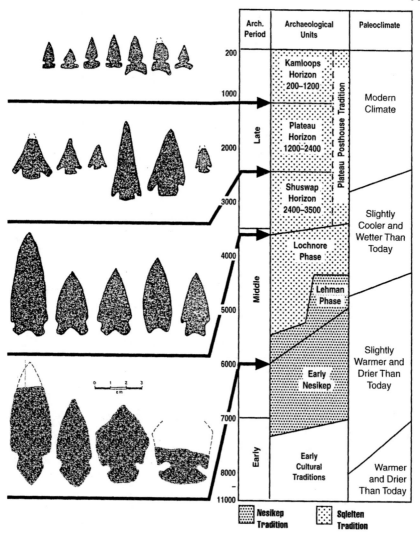

FIGURE 3.6. *A general chronological chart for the Canadian Plateau showing some of the changes in projectile point styles that occurred during the main periods of occupation (After Richards & Rousseau, 1987; Stryd & Rousseau, 1995).*

we began, there were few people who thought that isolating the living floors in housepits would be possible. They said there would be so much mixing and contamination that no meaningful conclusions could be drawn from such a study. Therefore, in our first season, it was extremely gratifying to actually see distinct layers of 3–5 cm thick sediments resting directly on sterile till within some housepit depressions. These few bottom centimeters looked and felt different from the mass of overlying dirt which we believed represented roof deposits (see Figure 3.4).

Finally, the housepit testing program confirmed the basic assumptions we had made about the nature of the structures at the site using historical and ethnographic

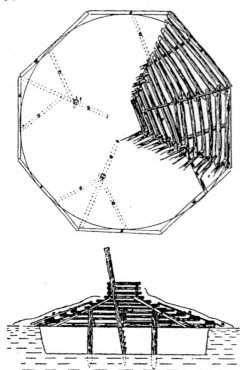

FIGURE 3.7A. *Dawson (1892) illustrated the construction details of these houses among the Shurwap (lower left) while Teit (1906) showed how sleeping benches and storage racks were traditionally constructed among the Lower Lillooet (below, right). Similar furniture is reported to have been used in pithouses.*

documents. That is, people dug shallow, flat-bottomed pits into the ground, then erected a timber roof frame over the pit which was covered with dirt (primarily for insulation), as described by James Teit (1900) and others (Figure 3.7A, B). In the course of our excavations, we discovered many details that did not conform to the ethnographic description of these houses, but the basic house model was corroborated.

Given the results from our testing program, it was possible to choose a number of housepits for more extensive excavation. My goal was to fully excavate the floor of at least one large, one medium-sized, and one small housepit. This obviously did not constitute a large enough sample from which to make statements about all large, medium, and small housepits at the site, but it did provide an initial indication as to what

FIGURE 3.7B. *A photograph of one of the few remaining pithouses at the turn of the century. Note in particular the earth covering and notched log ladder.*

those differences might well be like. Moreover, on the basis of our test trenches in other large and small houses at the site, it seems that the distinctive characteristics we identified from extensive excavations of large versus small housepits are also reflected in the other tested large versus small houses. In fact, we were able to excavate two additional small housepits, which provided a better appreciation of their variability. I feel relatively confident that the "small" versus "large" differences that will be discussed in the following chapters actually do characterize small versus large pithouses at the site.

We excavated each house in squares only 50 by 50 cm. This enabled us to control stratigraphic changes more accurately than larger excavation units would have permitted. Excavating in such small units also enabled us to create detailed distribution maps of artifacts across the living floors without having to record the precise coordinates of each object. For recording purposes, 16 of these 50 cm squares were grouped together to form a larger 2 by 2 m square. Each housepit was completely gridded in this fashion so it was possible to identify the artifacts' vertical position (by the different strata and level in which they occurred) and their horizontal position (by the square and subsquare in which they occurred). Soil samples were taken from all floor deposits at regular intervals for flotation involving the recovery of botanical remains, small faunal remains, and small lithic debris.

From the outset, we expected that if there were developed social and economic inequalities at Keatley Creek, these would be apparent in the differences between housepits in prestige items such as nephrite tools (nephrite is very similar to jade), copper and shell jewelry, or carved bone and stone. We also hoped to detect some differences in the use of economic resources such as fish versus deer and different storage capabilities. Finally, we hoped that social and economic divisions within the largest houses might be detectable using the same criteria. Traditionally, the grave goods associated with burials have constituted some of the best evidence for social and economic inequalities in past societies. However, we did not know where the cemetery for Keatley Creek was and we were not prepared to deal with the many complexities involved in excavating burials. In short, locating burials was not one of our goals.

FORMATION PROCESSES

Michael Schiffer (1987) and many others since have stressed the importance of understanding how artifact-bearing deposits form to clearly understand what archaeological objects represent and what biases might be present in the remains we study. For example, objects found inside house depressions might have been left by inhabitants fleeing a fire, or by neighborhood children using abandoned structures to play in, or by neighbors dumping refuse in abandoned houses. The objects might also have been artifacts from earlier occupations that had been accidentally introduced into later occupations as roofing material that collapsed, or they might simply represent the refuse existing in the house at the time it was abandoned. By studying formation processes, we can tell which scenario corresponds to particular deposits being excavated. To determine whether the floor deposits at Keatley Creek were authentic and to be able to interpret the remains from the site in social and economic terms, it was clearly necessary to understand how our archaeological deposits came to be created. We therefore embarked on a relatively detailed study of how deposits at Keatley Creek were formed. Some of these interpretations were straightforward and required little special analysis. Others were much more complicated.

Till

For instance, from geological work done in the area by June Ryder (1978) and others, it was relatively clear that the sterile deposits underlying the housepits were composed of *till* deposited by glaciers, the upper layers of which had been slightly weathered and become indurated from the leaching and subsequent precipitation of salts. About 20–30 cm of windblown silt, or loess, had been deposited on top of this till and periodically was swept up by high winds and redeposited.

When people built their houses, they removed this loess and dug down varying depths into the till. They piled this dug-out material around their housepit and used it to cover their roofs (Figure 3.8). Frequently, some of this dug up "sterile" material occurs at the base of housepit rims, but is less consolidated than the undisturbed, sterile till material and has an occasional piece of charcoal or stone flake in it.

Floors

In the course of excavating through roof, floor, and till deposits, we made numerous observations indicating that the living floor deposits were derived largely from the underlying till. Some of the intense, black organic staining that characterized many parts of floors was observed extending underneath cobbles that were clearly embedded in their original position within the till matrix. Patches of silt that occurred naturally within the till also typified the floor deposits immediately overlying them, but differed from the gravel-rich roof deposits that lay on top of the floor deposits. The view that floor sediments were essentially derived from the underlying till makes sense because after people had dug out the pit for their house, they would have begun to walk over the fresh till floor, scuffing up gravel and pebbles, and gradually creating a loose matrix that could easily incorporate small objects, ash, charcoal, and other material residues from various activities carried out within the house. However, there is more to the origin of floor deposits. Most floor deposits have reduced gravel contents compared to roof or till deposits. It appears that either gravel was being removed during housecleaning, or that fine silts and sands were being introduced into the houses by winds or by filtering through the roof onto the floor. The intense dark color of most floors, especially near hearth areas, almost certainly results from the grinding of charcoal underfoot as people walked across the floor and from other small organic wastes that decomposed within the floor sediments.

As might be expected, all the bones and stone tools found in the floor deposits displayed few indications of weathering. In fact, salmon ribs were still flexible and springy after more than a thousand years in the ground. When the houses were still standing, these materials were protected from sun and rain inside the houses, and when the roofs collapsed, the dirt on the roofs covered the floors, thereby sealing the deposits and helping to preserve bone and plant remains over the centuries.

One of the most important aspects of studying formation processes is to understand what objects have been brought into a depositional context, what objects have been removed from deposits to be discarded at a distance, and what objects have remained in the deposits. We will discuss what objects were brought into the housepits in the following chapters. Here it is sufficient to note that analysis of all the deposits associated with each housepit indicates the materials left in the floors seem representative of all the types of materials generated by the inhabitants with two special exceptions. First, items of great value (sculptures, jewelry, nephrite adzes) were taken away to other locations or buried with their owners and thus are rare in floor deposits. Second, most whole or useful tools were simply carried around until broken or used up and so there are few whole tools in floor deposits. On the other hand, some whole and useful items of little value such as large anvil stones and bulky, but easily made, spall tools were left inside the houses. A number of broken tools were also stored under beds. This is similar to how modern children often build up middens of unwanted or broken toys and objects under their beds, and to how homeowners store broken tools in corners of garages or basements in the hope that someday they might be of use. I refer to these types of items as "provisionally discarded" items. Since they are of little value, they are frequently left behind when houses are abandoned.

The rarity of valuable items and serviceable tools in the floor deposits at Keatley Creek indicates that the houses were not abandoned in a rush, since people typically leave many useful or valuable items behind if fire or warfare causes them to abandon their houses. There were no skeletons found to indicate violence or calamities and there were no charred posts in most of the postholes. Because the roof superstructures in the housepits we tested had been burned in the great majority of cases, the absence

Formation Processes for Mat-Roofed Pithouses

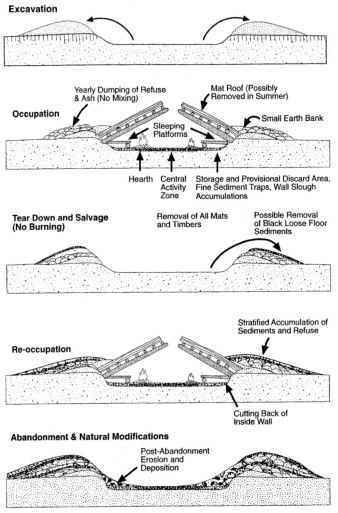

FIGURE 3.8. *A schematic illustration of the formation of roof and rim deposits over several cycles of roof replacements. Important differences in formation processes and deposit characteristics depended on whether the roofs of structures were mat covered or earth covered. Rim deposits of mat covered structures retained the stratified features of the deposited refuse, whereas the moving and churning of dirt for roofs in earth-covered houses generally destroyed stratification of refuse depostis in the rim. Medium and large housepits display a progression from clearly stratified rim deposits in lower levels to homogenized, churned deposits in the upper levels indicating a change from mat-covered to earth-covered roofs probably around 1,500 years ago.*

of large charred beams and center posts indicates that the main support posts and beams had been deliberately removed before the houses had been burned. The occurrence of the smaller, charred cross-beams and thin layers of charcoal lying on top of the floor deposits indicates that these roofs were burned soon after the residents had

Formation Processes for Earth-Roofed Pithouses

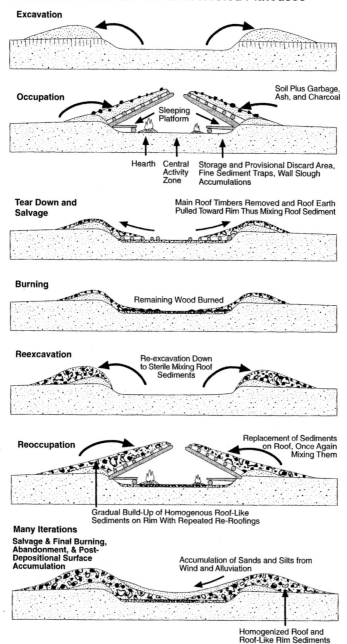

In each re-roofing cycle of earth-covered houses, refuse accumulated on the roof and on the rim during occupation. All this material was then piled on the rims while the old roof was being replaced, and much of the soil and refuse from the previous occupations was then thrown on top of the new roof or left churned up on the rims. In this way, increasing amounts mixed together and accumulated over time in the roof deposits and in the portion of the rim affected by reroofing activities.

left; that is, not enough time had elapsed to allow the roofs to collapse even partially from rotting.

Thus, the objects left in the floor deposits were either of little value to the inhabitants or objects that were small and had been lost. Although we tested other areas of the site to determine if there were garbage dump locations, such as pits or abandoned houses, we did not find any indication that the dumping of garbage took place to any significant degree away from the houses where it was produced. Given the very cold temperatures of Lillooet winters, it is not surprising that people generally dumped their garbage as close as possible, notably, out the door.

Finally, most of the houses we tested had only 3–5 cm of floor deposits laying over the sterile till, and these floors always had projectile points in them from the last occupation period of the house. It seems clear that when the inhabitants replaced the roofs of the houses (probably every 10 to 20 years—Condrashoff, 1972, 1980) they cleaned out all of the loose floor deposits that had accumulated over the previous 20 years and dumped them around the edge of the housepit. Later this material would be incorporated into the dirt heaped on the newly constructed roof (see Figure 3.8).

Roofs

It is obvious the roof deposits are derived from till because the percentage of sand, silt, and gravel in the roof deposits is almost identical to the underlying till. While there are some oral accounts of people bringing in clay or silt to cover their roofs, there is little evidence that anyone at Keatley Creek did this a thousand and more years ago. However, there is more to the roofs than just sand, silt, and gravel. The roof deposits have a distinctive, dark gray color and contain artifacts, bones, and carbonized plant remains that do not occur in the till. As already noted, there is a range of color from brown to almost black depending upon the housepit size; and there is a similar range in artifact, bone, and carbonized plant material density, from extremely sparse occurrences among some of the smaller housepits to the extremely dense occurrences of larger housepits. Moreover, there is no stratification of deposits in the roof materials such as in the rim deposits of larger houses.

The varying and sometimes dark color of the roof can be easily explained in terms of waste organic materials accumulating and decaying in these sediments. These materials probably included human wastes, discarded plant remains, discarded animal wastes (bone fragments, spilled fats, hair), and certainly ashes and charcoal powder or bits. The longer a house was used, the more this organic material was incorporated into the roof deposits. However, it was not clear whether these materials, as well as the bone and stone waste (a) were thrown onto the roof as garbage cleaned out from the house interiors, (b) whether they were waste products from activities performed on the roof, or (c) whether they were incidentally incorporated into the roof deposits when the roof was replaced and floor deposits were cleaned out only to become mixed with the soil used on the new roof.

Therefore, we conducted a series of analyses comparing the breakage state of stone tools, the wear state of tools, the weathering state of tools, the density of tools, the relative frequencies of different types of stone tools, and the spatial distribution of tools from the roof and floor deposits. From these analyses, it was clear the stone tools

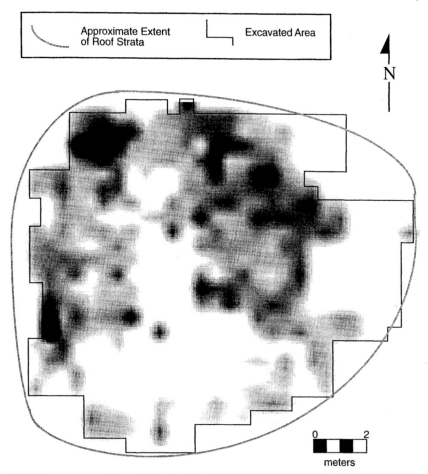

FIGURE 3.9. *Distribution of fire-cracked rocks in the roof of Housepit 7. Note the strong concentration of these objects in the northeast side of the house where it would have been coldest and the roof would have been least likely to be used during the day.*

and their conditions in the roof were almost identical to the tools in the floors, except that the tools in the roof exhibited slightly more staining and weathering. Types and proportions of stone waste materials, or debitage, were also very similar. Thus it became evident that either people were cleaning up their waste materials and throwing them on the roof, or that everything that was being incorporated into the floor deposits was subsequently incorporated into the roof deposits during reroofing events.

On the other hand, there was also some evidence from the spatial distributions that at least some roof areas were probably used for special activities, notably in the southwest sectors where the afternoon sun was warmest and in the northeast sector, which had the most shade. The northeast areas may actually have been used as butchering areas and as special dumping areas for cumbersome types of garbage, such as fire-cracked rock (Figure 3.9). Large bones and fire-cracked rocks are found concentrated in the northeast in several housepit roofs. But the contribution of these specialized activity areas and refuse dumping areas to the artifacts contained in the roof assemblage as a whole is swamped by the great quantity of everyday garbage incorporated into the roofs.

It is reasonable to assume that other bone and plant material was treated like the stone material, however, two processes have reduced their visibility in the roof deposits. First, being thrown onto the surface of the roof would have rendered organic objects susceptible to decay from exposure to the elements and pulverization from foot traffic as well as to scavenging from dogs, rodents, or birds. Second, the fact that roof deposits were periodically churned up during the reroofing of houses would have cycled many buried elements to the surface where they would tend to decay, as well as grinding up fragile elements. These inferences are supported by the lower density and frequency of the more fragile types of bone remains in the roof deposits, compared to floor and rim deposits, as well as by the notably weathered nature of almost all faunal remains recovered from the roof deposits versus the almost pristine, unweathered condition of most bone elements recovered from the floors. The homogenous nature of the roof deposits also testifies to the periodic churning that must have occurred.

Rims

In the case of small houses, it is clear that the rims were simply extensions of the dirt covering the roof; these rims had all the same characteristics as the roof sediments. In the case of the thick rim middens of large housepits, there appeared to be something different involved since there were remarkably thick deposits of organic materials, alternating with lenses of till, or charcoal, or discolored sand and gravel. The nature of the thin, limited lenses made it apparent that they were dumps of waste material or soils from inside the houses that had been removed in the excavation of storage pits or other renovations. The dumping of large amounts of plant materials appeared to be major events, such as might occur during renovations or once a year when the previous year's dried conifer needles, grasses, and other plant wastes would be cleaned out of the house before moving in for the winter. The thick and rapid buildup of these materials on the rim together with the downcurved surface of the rim all seems to have helped shed rainwater and helped keep the inside of these rims remarkably dry, thus helping preserve the plant materials inside them. However, as with the roof, we also discovered evidence for special areas of the rim being used for flintknapping or the special discard of lithic materials.

SUMMARY

The study of site formation processes has enabled us to determine several important facts. It has demonstrated that the houses at Keatley Creek were abandoned in a planned and systematic fashion. It has also demonstrated that there are no significant differences between types of deposits in terms of the types of refuse or material remains left behind. Exceptions involve a high concentration of preserved plant material in the rims, the poor preservation of bone materials in the roof deposits, and the concentration inside the houses of provisionally discarded or bulky items of little worth such as anvils and abrading stones. However, these objects were of great importance from the perspective of the goals of the project, as we shall see.

The study of formation processes also indicated that there were some very important differences between floor deposits and roof deposits. The floors had less gravel; the bones and carbonized plant remains in floor deposits were better preserved and more abundant than in the roof; the floors mirrored localized changes in the texture of underlying till deposits rather than resembling the overlying roof deposits; and the floors were frequently covered by burned beams or thin charcoal layers. We also examined the angle, or dip, of artifacts found in roof and floor deposits and found that artifacts in roof deposits exhibited more random orientations, occurring vertically, horizontally and at oblique angles, as one might expect from churned up sediments; whereas there was a marked tendency for artifacts found in floor deposits to occur in horizontal positions.

This study of the formation of deposits at Keatley Creek therefore contributed a number of vital facts to our research. Of critical importance for the following chapters, it confirmed our initial impressions from the housepit testing program that at least in the houses we had selected for excavation, it was possible to successfully distinguish floor from roof deposits. Therefore, our hope of being able to recover some patterns from the floors that could indicate the nature of social and economic organization inside the houses was considerably strengthened. But until we had completed the excavation program and actually analyzed the stones and bones and plants from the floors, we would not really know if we could say anything about any aspect of organized behavior inside the housepits at the site. The intervening years of analysis were frustratingly long, and many people devoted a great deal of time to pursing this question. Our efforts were well rewarded, as readers may appreciate in the following chapters.

CHAPTER 4
What the Features Revealed

Archaeological features consist of everything that cannot be picked up and carried away. They are usually modifications to the earth, but can also be objects in special relationships, such as teepee rings or alignments of objects. A great deal can be learned about past cultures simply from studying the features at a site. At Keatley Creek, there are five basic types of features: house or structure depressions, storage pits, hearths, postholes, and roasting pits. Some other types of features that we will not discuss in detail include benches inside houses, small pits, and small structures. There also appear to be large earthen ramps associated with the entrances to the site areas at both the Keatley Creek and the Bell sites, as well as an earth ramp leading up to the suspected ritual areas on the highest terrace at Keatley Creek. Unfortunately, we have not had time to investigate these very large features to verify that they are man-made (or modified) features. Let us begin by examining the most obvious type of feature at the site, the housepits, to see what they can reveal about the prehistoric community.

HOUSEPITS

Housepits can open up a surprising number of insights into past cultures all on their own. They provide estimates for population sizes of individual structures as well as entire sites. They can tell us about the degree of equality or hierarchy in sites and about how groups were organized. Also, together with information from postholes, they constitute the basis for understanding the architecture of the structures.

Until recently, there were a number of formulas archaeologists used to estimate the number of square meters of living space used per person in traditional societies. These estimates were based on worldwide ethnographic observations and indicated that on average each person had 10 square meters of floorspace. The few estimates that James Teit provided for the number of inhabitants in the pithouses he described did not correspond very well with the formulas used by most archaeologists. I began to suspect that pithouses might constitute a special category of dwellings in this respect. Together with several students, and Dr. Gregory Reinhardt who had studied Arctic housing, we began to collect all the observations we could, from Alaska to California, on pithouse sizes and the number of inhabitants that lived in them. When we assembled all of these observations, it was clear that people who lived in housepits had much less floor space than people living in other types of dwellings

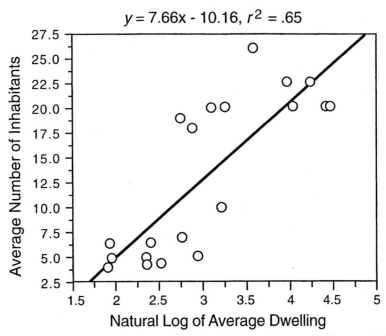

$$y = 7.66x - 10.16, r^2 = .65$$

FIGURE 4.1. *This graph shows the number of inhabitants ethnographically recorded as living in winter semisubterranean houses plotted against the recorded floor area of these houses. The average is about 2 to 3 square meters of floor area per person.*

throughout the world. People in pithouses averaged only 2–3 square meters of floorspace per person (Figure 4.1). This estimate corresponded much better with Teit's observations. Such a dense press of people is unthinkable for today's industrial citizen. For personal interest, try to estimate the amount of floorspace per person you have in your home. Then measure the room you are in to determine how many people would live in it if it were a pithouse.

Under traditional conditions, the high density of people in pithouses made a great deal of sense. The prime goal of pithouse living was to survive the winter, and pithouses, as a labor intensive type of shelter, make most sense in environments with severe winters. If stored food with lots of calories was necessary to survive the winter, so was staying warm. Pithouses were relatively well-insulated from the cold by the earthen floors and walls, and the earth-covered roofs; but pithouses also required a source of heat to remain comfortable. It appears that for daily heating, most groups relied to a large extent on the body heat given off by the pithouse's closely packed residents, similar to the effects of partygoers heating up crowded rooms.

Bolstered by the knowledge that Teit was not in error or unique in his observations on the density of people living in pithouses, but was consistent with all the other observations made of housepit residents, we were able to confidently estimate the number of people in each housepit by calculating its floor area (Table 4.1), and we were also able to estimate the population for the entire site (Table 4.2). As will be explained in chapter 8, we had good reasons to assume the great majority of the large- and medium-sized housepits were occupied throughout the history of the site,

TABLE 4.1
POPULATION ESTIMATES OF INDIVIDUAL HOUSEPITS

House Radius (m)	Floor Area (m²)	Pithouse Population									
2.50	19.6	19	13	9	7	6	5	4	4	3	
3.00	28.3	28	18	14	11	9	8	7	6	5	
3.50	38.5	38	<u>25</u>	<u>19</u>	15	12	10	9	8	7	HP 12
4.00	50.3	50	33	25	20	16	14	12	11	10	
4.50	63.6	63	42	31	25	21	18	15	14	12	
5.00	78.5	78	52	<u>39</u>	**31**	26	22	19	17	15	HP 3
5.50	95.0	95	63	<u>47</u>	38	31	27	23	21	19	
6.00	113.1	113	75	56	**45**	37	32	28	25	22	HP 7
6.50	132.7	132	88	<u>66</u>	53	44	37	33	29	26	
7.00	153.9	153	102	76	61	51	43	38	34	30	
m²/person		1	1.5	2	2.5	3	3.5	4	4.5	5	

Note. Pithouse populations for the relevant range of floor areas and population densities. The underlined values show the range of the best estimates for the populations of the housepits indicated in the right margin, with the most probable value printed in bold type. From Spafford, 1991.

TABLE 4.2
POPULATION ESTIMATES FOR KEATLEY CREEK

1. Assuming there is a linear relationship between rim and floor diameter, and based on the data from HPs 12, 3, and 7, the following regression formula was generated:

floor diameter = 2.7 + 0.47 (rim diameter)

2. Population density is assumed to be higher in smaller housepits. Figures used for density estimates were:

large HPs = 2.5 m²/person

small HPs = 2 m²/person

3. Excavated housepits with diameters > 14 m (*n* = 6) consistently have evidence of occupations extending across at least two Plateau Pithouse horizons. Evidence of occupation during three or even four horizons is present in four out of the six. So, large housepits were probably occupied throughout much of the site's history.

Smaller housepits tend to have shorter occupations. Probably only a portion of small housepits were occupied at any given time. Thus the estimated population of large and medium HPs = 1,100; with 1/4 of small HPs = 1,500 total site population, or with 1/2 of small HPs = 1,900 total site population.

and the more ephemeral smaller houses probably were most numerous during the Plateau Horizon. In any event, a good proportion (we assumed 25%) of the smaller houses were probably occupied simultaneously at the peak of the site's growth. The fact that there is little overlap of housepits at Keatley Creek is one indication that a large percentage of these structures were occupied simultaneously. Even using the

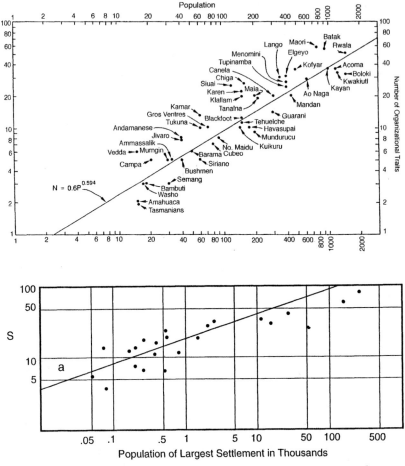

FIGURE 4.2. *Two studies show the relationship between the population sizes of communities and their relative complexity. The graph at the top was compiled by Robert Carneiro (1967) and demonstrates how overall social complexity increases with community size. Earlier, Raoul Naroll (1956, p. 689) documented a similar relationship for types of social organizations and the size of the largest settlement, and in addition he showed that the number of occupational specialists was also related to the size of the largest settlement in a similar fashion (bottom graph). Clark and Parry (1990) subsequently confirmed this result. On the basis of these studies, Keatley Creek, with a population of 1,200, should have had about 20 occupational specialties (including corporate administrators, shamans, warriors, hunters, carvers, and others), and it should have had about 10 different types of social organizations (including nuclear families, lineages, clans, corporate groups, dance societies, elite secret societies, work groups, and others).*

more conservative estimates of floor space per person and the number of housepits occupied at any one time, the peak population of the community at Keatley Creek must have been at least 1,200 to 1,500 people. This number of people, as well as the area covered by the entire site (the densely settled core of the site covers 4 hectares [ha], while the overall site spreads out to about 12 ha), would be grounds for calling

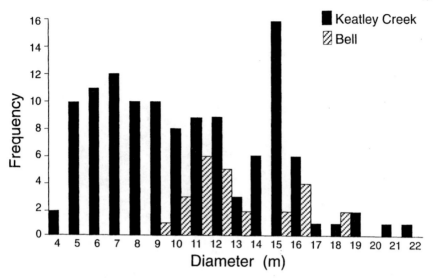

FIGURE 4.3. *A histogram showing the size distribution of housepits at the Keatley Creek site and at the Bell site. Note the two pronounced peaks that occur in both distributions. There may even be a third peak at 19 m for the largest houses at Keatley Creek. Housepit size was measured from rim crest to rim crest.*

Keatley Creek a "town" rather than a village in many archaeological approaches. For instance, Adams and Nissen (1972, p. 18) define towns as sites larger than 6 ha.

Estimating the number of people living at Keatley Creek is very important for understanding the social and economic complexity of the site because a number of anthropological studies have shown that as communities increase in size, so do their number of specialized political, economic, social, and other roles and institutions (Figure 4.2). Although not foolproof, this is an important initial indicator that the community at Keatley Creek was relatively complex. Indicative of this complexity is the fact that *all* the people of a typical generalized hunter–gatherer community (i.e., about 25 to 50 people) would equal the number of residents in a *single* medium-sized housepit at Keatley Creek. The full community of Keatley Creek at its height could have been 60 times larger than the average community of generalized hunter–gatherers.

Still another indicator of complexity is furnished by examining the distribution of housepit sizes. At Keatley Creek, as at the neighboring Bell site, there are few large housepits, but they form a distinct peak at one end of the size spectrum resulting in a *bimodal* distribution, that is, a distribution with two peaks (Figure 4.3). This indicates that there are two distinct groups of housepits and residents at Keatley Creek: the more ordinary ones living in housepits up to 13 m in diameter, and the unusual ones living in housepits up to 22 m in diameter.

However, the mere occurrence of large-sized housepits by themselves does not indicate there were inequalities. They could simply represent one end of an egalitarian-size continuum. It is the distinctiveness of the large housepits as a group, separate from the others, that indicates the presence of inequalities. This is why the bimodal

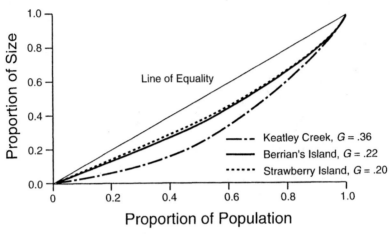

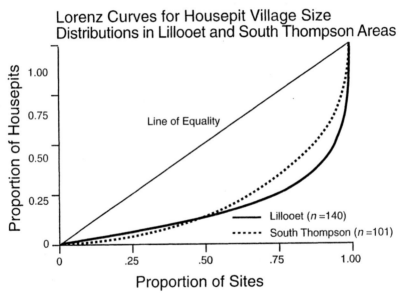

FIGURE 4.4. *The graph at top displays Lorenz curves showing the degree of departure from an ideal egalitarian distribution of the housepit sizes at Keatley Creek and two other sites from the Columbia Plateau (Berrian's Island and Strawberry Island added for comparative purposes). Thus, not all Plateau housepit sites seem to have exhibited the same degree of hierarchical organization and inequality. On a regional level, the bottom graph shows that hierarchical organization between sites in the Mid-Fraser and South Thompson River areas may have been even more pronounced (Gini indices for these areas are 0.64 and 0.57 respectively), although these results may partially reflect temporal mixing of sites from different time periods.*

shape of the pithouse size distribution is important. Another means of measuring inequality in size distributions or other data is provided by Lorenz curves and Gini indices. Using these techniques, the size of each housepit is plotted on a graph from smallest to largest, and the resulting shape of the curve indicates how much inequality is present in the distribution (Figure 4.4).

If the large housepits had simply been one end of a regular continuum, the graph curve would have been a straight line, and they would have scored a 0 on the Gini index. If there had been complete inequality, or hierarchy in the distribution, the figure would have been very concave, and the Gini index would register close to 1.0. By using Lorenz curves and the Gini index to gauge the degree of inequality in housepit sizes at Keatley Creek, Rick Schulting was able to show that there is a considerable degree of inequality present, registering 0.36 on the Gini index. This, too, is an important indication that there were relatively complex social and economic relationships present in the prehistoric Keatley Creek community. It is interesting to note that the largest housepits at the site are spread out evenly in the site's core, almost as if each large house dominated a neighborhood, or was allied with its own group of neighboring houses (refer to Figure 3.3).

If we look at a broader regional picture of site sizes (see Figure 4.4), these, too, display a significant degree of hierarchy. The values derived from the Fraser Valley near Lillooet and the South Thompson River Valley sites are 0.64 and 0.57 respectively. These surprisingly high figures may be due in part to the inclusion of some undated sites from different time periods. But clearly, there is very substantial inequality between communities at the regional level as well. Such hierarchies characterize increasingly complex social organizations with different levels of wealth and power. Thus, site population estimates, the distribution of housepit sizes, and the regional distribution of site sizes all point to an important conclusion: The residents of Keatley Creek formed part of a complex society with fairly important inequalities, hierarchies, and specialization within communities. Analysis by Rick Schuting (1995) of burials recovered from the Plateau area also show similar degrees of inequality in burial items to the Lorenz curves of the Lillooet housepits.

HEARTHS

Let us take a detailed look at some of the features inside a few of these houses. In the smallest houses, such as Housepits 12 and 90, there is almost no trace of a detectable hearth (Figure 4.5). Only a small, thin patch of fire-reddened till and a sparse scatter of fire-cracked rocks betrays the presence of a hearth in Housepit 12. It does not appear to have been used very often, nor for very long times, or built up into a very large fire. There was not even a detectable ash accumulation over the fire-reddened area, which indicates the hearth area had not been used for some time prior to abandonment of the pithouse, but instead had been used as a normal part of the floor for walking on. Housepit 90 had no detectable hearth area. Thus, it seems that in the small houses we excavated, residents relied primarily on body warmth to heat the interior of their houses and used fires only for special occasions or during intensely cold nights in winter. Such strategies may have been due to poor ventilation within pithouses and the dangers of smoke poisoning, or they may have been related to the exhaustion of the firewood supply within walking radius of the community. At this point, we do not know.

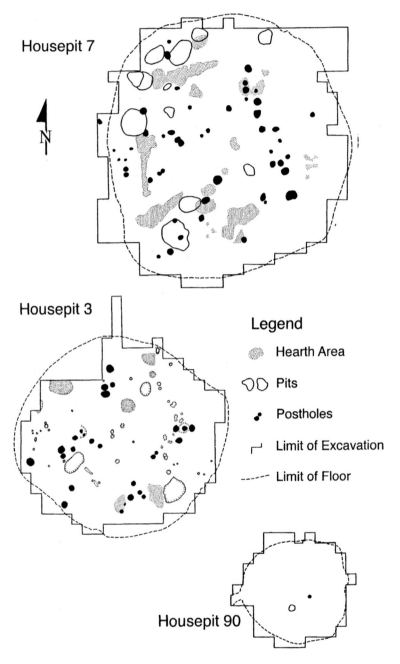

FIGURE 4.5. *Floor plans of a large housepit (HP 7), a medium-sized housepit (HP 3), and a small housepit (HP 90). Note in particular the lack of main postholes, storage pits, and fire-reddening in the small housepit compared to the regular and pronounced development of these features in the large housepit. This implies that fires were used infrequently in smaller houses and were much smaller than in large houses. Note also the small side entrance on the left side of HP 90.*

In contrast to the small houses, the larger houses such as Housepit 7 have a number of large, deeply reddened (up to 8 cm into the till) hearth areas that form an inner ring about 2 m inside the house wall (Figure 4.5). This suggests considerably more use of hearths with larger and more lasting fires in the larger houses than in the smaller houses. Concentrations of fire-cracked rocks near the hearths also suggest more cooking activity than in the smaller houses. However, even in the larger houses, most of the hearths lacked accumulations of ash above the fire-reddened areas indicating that they, too, had been used primarily for special events or only on the coldest nights. Otherwise the hearth areas were simply used as normal floor space for walking and other activities. The lack of ash is so consistent a pattern in the housepits we excavated and tested that this intermittent use of hearths seems to be a general feature of pithouse life at Keatley Creek. The lack of evidence for any activities in the housepits just prior to abandonment, other than the routine daily activities, reinforces the notion that the condition of the hearths as we found them was a normal one.

However, there is something else interesting that you may have already noticed about the hearth areas in Figure 4.5. Even without information on the depth of fire-reddening, it is apparent that the hearth areas on the left half of Housepit 7 are much larger and more numerous than those on the right side of the house. It is on the left side, too, that fire reddening is deep, whereas the fire reddening of hearths on the right side of the house was more superficial, at most 2 cm deep. The patterning is clear, but the reason for the patterning is not so clear. The two most probable reasons for the hearths being different on the two sides of the house include (1) different activities being conducted on the two sides of the houses, for instance, eating on one side of the house versus sleeping on the other; or (2) the hearths could differ because of the characteristics of the families residing on the two sides of the house, such as poor families on one side versus wealthy families on the other side. This is a fundamental question about the social and economic organization of these large houses that will require many different types of evidence to adequately address: It requires evidence from other features, from food remains, from remains of stone tools, and from plant remains. Let us look at the remaining features first.

PIT FEATURES

Relatively large storage pits have been found inside some of the tested and excavated housepits at Keatley Creek. Similar storage pits are also found between houses and in special areas on the peripheries of the site. The storage pits inside houses vary in depth from about 30 cm to over a meter below the floors. Ethnographically, they are described as used for storing dried salmon, meat, berries, and roots. James Teit called them "cellars," but he makes it clear that he is talking about pits covered with poles or boards. We know the archaeological examples were used in a similar fashion because in the bottom sediments of some of these large pits we have found layers of articulated salmon backbones laid one next to another, or in other cases, layers of disarticulated salmon bones at the bottoms of pits.

The occurrence of large storage pits in some houses but not others provides an important clue as to the nature of past social and economic organization at the site. With few exceptions, the smaller houses had only small or no food storage pits (see

Figure 4.5). By contrast, the large housepit we excavated had numerous, large storage pits (Figure 4.6) and the other large housepits we tested also contained large storage pits (see Figure 3.4). If we calculate the storage volume per square meter of floor area for each house, this is almost the same as calculating the amount of storage per person for each house. Can you see why this is so? When this is done, it can be seen that Housepit 7, the large house, has far more storage capacity per unit floor area and per person than any of the smaller houses (Table 4.3). If we examine the total volume of storage pits in each house, the contrast between large and small

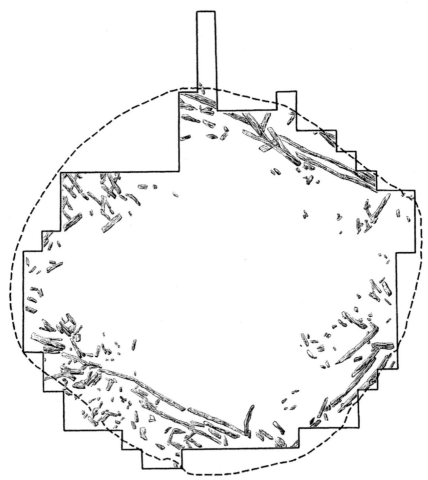

FIGURE 4.6. *Charred roof beams found lying on the floor of Housepit 3. Note that only the thinner secondary cross-beams are represented and that none of the heavier and thicker major joists or support posts are present. Since these heavier beams should have burned much slower and been better preserved than the lighter cross-beams, it seems that all the heavier timbers were removed from the structure prior to its burning.*

TABLE 4.3

STORAGE CAPACITY OF LARGE STORAGE PITS BY HOUSEPIT

HP 12 Feature Number	Depth	Diameter	Estimated Volume	
P-2	70	94		485.78
P-3	35	65		116.14
P-5	35	40		43.98
			Total storage volume	771.91
			Estimated floor area	38.50
			Liters storage / m² floor	**20.05**

HP 3 Feature Number	Depth	Diameter	Estimated Volume	
HP 3-89:2	76	114		775.73
P-1	44	58		116.25
P-2	145	114		495.90
P-3	44	102		359.54
			Total storage volume	1747.42
			Estimated floor area	78.50
			Liters storage / m² floor	**22.26**

HP 7 Feature Number	Depth	Diameter	Estimated Volume	
P-4	65	156		1242.37
P-2	120	113		1203.45
P-25	100	130		1327.32
P-31	115	135		1646.10
89-5	130	101		1041.54
P-36A	75	81		386.47
P-34	55	80		276.46
P-4	60	87		356.68
P-36	60	72		244.29
P-35B	32	90		203.58
			Storage volume: large pits	6460.78
			Estimated floor area	113.10
			Liters storage / m² floor	57.12
			Storage volume: large and medium pits	7928.26
			Estimated floor area	113.10
			Liters storage / m² floor	**70.10**

HP 3 Feature Number	Depth	Diameter	Estimated Volume	
P-1	82	126		1022.46
			Estimated floor area	20.5
			Liters storage / m² floor	**49.88**

houses is even more striking. This seems to indicate that residents of larger houses had a great deal more surplus food than residents of smaller houses.

But there is more evidence to be gleaned from these prehistoric cellars located inside the houses. Can you detect any patterning to the occurrence of storage pits inside Housepit 7? A careful scrutiny of Figure 4.5 reveals that virtually all of the large storage pits in the house are located in the left half of the floor, with none occurring on the right side. Moreover, the storage pits seem to be closely associated with the large hearths in the house which also occur on the left side of the floor. Once again, we are faced with a fundamental question in trying to understand the past social and economic organization within these structures. There is obviously a strong pattern to the location of storage pits inside the large house. But is the patterning of storage pits and hearths on the left side of the house due to activity differences between the left and right sides of the house (for instance, food storage and cooking occurring on the left), or does it indicate differences in storage activities between families living on the left side of the house (presumably the wealthier families) versus families on the right side (presumably the poorer families)? Although we have not yet finished accumulating observations to decide whether activities or socioeconomic differences are responsible for this patterning, you may have already begun to form an opinion. Which do you think is more likely? Are there any arguments you can think of at this point to support your opinion? What further kinds of observations do you think would help resolve this issue? One clue might be found in the distribution of the fire-cracked rocks mentioned during the discussion of formation processes.

POSTHOLES

In most traditional societies around the world, people dig narrow holes in which to place support posts for their structures, and sometimes holes are used to construct internal post partitions or for furniture, such as benches or beds. Virtually all of the postholes that we found at Keatley Creek were vertical to the floor, not angled as James Teit indicated in his ethnographic illustrations of housepits. Placing posts in holes stabilizes them and prevents them from being knocked over or slipping out of place with potentially disastrous results. Thus, holes are commonly dug for structural posts, although some special types of architecture and furniture use only posts placed on the surface of the floor. We will first examine the main support posts used to hold up the large roof beams in houses.

The holes for the main support posts were dug deep into the clean, yellow till— as far as people could reach with their arms. When the posts decayed or were removed, the postholes filled up with dark soil from the house floor or roof, thus making it very easy to recognize the postholes in the yellow till. Moreover, because of the depth of these holes, the traces of the earliest, first, postholes dug in the house floor are still visible, even after the progressive cleaning up of scuffed floor deposits when houses were reroofed.

As with any house that lasts more than a generation or two, it was possible to enlarge, reduce, or remodel the house to suit the needs of current generations, especially when the roof was replaced. However, the depth and distinctive color of the main deep postholes enable archaeologists to keep track of any changes in size or major structural remodeling that took place over the entire lifetime of a particular house.

While the same large postholes might be used for successive roof structures, it was probable that the shape of the trunks of the large trees used to make main support posts and main roof beams varied from one roofing event to the next, thereby making it necessary to slightly alter the positions of some postholes from time to time. But if the house did not change its basic size or structure throughout its lifetime, then all of these new, main support postholes should cluster around the locations of the original posts. This is clearly the case in Housepit 3 and in Housepit 7 (see Figure 4.5). If either of these structures had changed in size from their first construction in Shuswap times until their abandonment, well over 1,000 years later, this would have shown up in the pattern of remnant postholes visible in the till, although traces of very small previous houses might be obliterated. It seems clear that once firmly established, these larger houses remained the same basic size and adhered to the same basic design until they were abandoned, a conclusion indicated in our discussion of the formation of rim deposits in chapter 3. This seems to imply a continuity of use over a long period of time. The social and economic implications of such an observation may not be immediately apparent, but they are quite profound, as we shall see in chapter 8.

Astute readers might think hearths and storage pits could be used in similar ways to make inferences about the modifications to a structure over time. While the evidence from the hearths and storage pits in Housepits 3 and 7 do support the notion that these structures did not change in size or organization over time (the hearths and pits occur in a band with a constant distance of one to four meters from the wall of the house), skeptics could weaken such arguments. It could be argued, for instance, that all the evidence of previous hearths had been removed when scuffed up till and floor soils were removed with successive reroofing events, thus, gradually lowering the floor level. It could also be argued that the storage pits were all dug and used during a very short period of time, or at least only when the house was at its present size, during the final occupation. Although these lines of evidence are relevant to deciphering the life histories of houses and are consistent with other types of evidence, they are not as good indicators of house histories as deep postholes.

In addition to providing important information on the life history of structures, the study of postholes can provide a great deal of information about the nature of the superstructure of a housepit roof and about the arrangement of household activities. Contrary to what we expected from the ethnographies, not all housepits at Keatley Creek had the same kind of superstructure. For example, it came as a great surprise to find that most small housepits had no support posts at all. When I consulted Richard MacDonald, an architect, as to the likely nature of these houses, he began a series of possible architectural reconstructions based on evidence from postholes, as well as the pattern of the smaller burned roof beams that we had found lying on the floors (refer to Figure 4.6). Using this evidence, he was able to infer that small houses probably had roof slopes too steep to enter them from the smoke

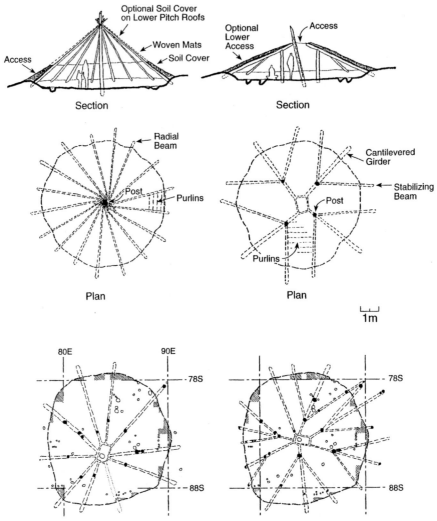

FIGURE 4.7. *Several of the possible architectural reconstructions formulated by Richard MacDonald for housepits based on the postholes and features associated with housepit floors and the application of architectural principles. In contrast to ethnographic descriptions, small houses probably had very steep roof pitches that made entry through the smoke hole impractical.*

hole as described ethnographically (see Figures 3.7, 4.7). In fact, once we began looking for side entrances in small houses, we began finding them (see Figure 4.5). The medium-sized houses with four main support posts corresponded closely to the descriptions and illustrations of housepits published by James Teit. On the other hand, the large houses, such as Housepit 7, presented still different architectural features, including probably six main support posts and secondary support posts near the walls. In addition, the smoke holes of the large houses would have been so high above the floor that it is difficult to imagine how small children, elderly, or sick individuals could have used the smoke holes to enter and leave the housepits without frequent accidents. We have not yet been able to identify a side entrance for Housepit 7 or any other large housepits, and it seems worth considering the possibility that a landing platform may have existed under the smoke hole, about halfway to the floor. A row of large postholes in this area may have supported such a platform (refer to Figure 4.5).

Aside from the main support posts, there was also an assortment of other post impressions in Housepits 3 and 7. The purpose of these is still enigmatic, but the occurrence of paired, small, shallow posts near the walls (not illustrated) may indicate the placements for poles that supported sleeping platforms, as described in the ethnographies.

Finally, although the actual posts had been removed from most main postholes, occasionally one or two had been left to burn in place. From the charred remains, it was possible for Dana Lepofsky, a botanical specialist, to determine the type of wood used for posts. I had fully expected Douglas fir to have been used because it is a stronger, denser, more rot-resistant wood. I was very surprised to learn that all the post remains that we recovered were actually pine (*Pinus ponderosa*). Since pine and Douglas fir both grow in the vicinity today and are both represented in charcoal samples taken from the floors of the housepits, it is clear that the prehistoric residents of Keatley Creek purposefully chose pine over fir for the largest posts. On the basis of experiments conducted with ground stone adzes, I suspected the reason they chose pine was that large pine trees were much easier to cut down using stone tools and resulted in less damage to the tools. Later, I read an unpublished manuscript of James Teit that confirmed this was indeed the case. The length of time the pine supports lasted was apparently of less importance than the risk of damaging tools or the relative ease of cutting the posts, perhaps because smaller elements of the roof would rot far before the main supports.

Thus, simple postholes have provided an important array of information about past life at Keatley Creek. They have revealed what kinds of structures were present, the life histories of those structures, something about the organization of activities within structures (the entrances and sleeping areas), and also something about the technology and concerns of the house builders.

ROASTING PITS

The last type of feature I will discuss is the roasting pit. These are shallow depressions usually filled with charcoal or ashy material, as well as fire-cracked rock, animal bones, or plant remains. Roasting pits are important because in a winter village site such as Keatley Creek, they may represent large-scale food preparation for unusually large gatherings of people at feasts. Roasting pits also occur in the mountains where large quantities of plant foods need to be cooked as part of the drying and preserving process. However, no large sources of plant foods requiring such processing are known for the immediate site area of Keatley Creek. Therefore, it seems likely that most, if not all, of the roasting pits at Keatley Creek are associated with feasting activities. A large roasting area is associated with Housepit 7, and there are surface indications that roasting pits may be associated with most or all of the other large housepits at the site. We have not detected any roasting pits associated with small housepits at Keatley Creek. We have also excavated several roasting pits associated with two very high, peripheral structures that may have been used for ritual feasting. Feasts will feature importantly in the concluding discussions about Keatley Creek.

SUMMARY

The seemingly simple study of site features has brought a wide array of issues before us, as well as some compelling reasons for viewing the Keatley Creek community as a relatively complex group of hunter–gatherers. On the basis of structural evidence and rim midden accumulations, Keatley Creek was certainly a large, seasonally reoccupied, semi-sedentary community. Population estimates, distributions of house sizes by rank and size, the differential occurrence of food storage and hearths, all suggest that inequalities in wealth and social roles were significant, and hierarchical and specialized roles were probably present in the prehistoric community at Keatley Creek throughout most of its occupation. We were also able to reconstruct the nature of the buildings people lived in and track the basic history of those buildings. Tangential observations point to the presence of feasting and a stone technology that probably had difficulty felling large, dense trees. Tantalizing patterns of hearth and pit features within the largest house studied reveal a strongly structured organization within this house, but we have still not been able to identify the source of that patterning. Let us turn to the artifactual evidence to determine whether artifact patterning can provide a more definitive answer.

CHAPTER 5

What the Stones Had to Say

There is a wide range of stone, or lithic, material at Keatley Creek. There are fire-cracked rocks, granite boulders used as anvils, sandstone slabs for sharpening bone awls, coarse quartzite spalls, cherts, fine-grained igneous rocks, obsidian, finely ground nephrite celts, mica sheets, ochres, and a number of specialty items including shaped graphite, hammered native copper, carved serpentine, shaped marble, and slate pendants. There is a great wealth of information derived from all these various materials. In this chapter, I will focus on some of the highlights.

TOOL FORMATION PROCESSES

Materials for heating rocks, anvils, and quartzite spalls were available in the immediate vicinity of Keatley Creek, either eroding from the till or from the glacial outwash terraces of the Fraser River. When people needed these materials, they simply went out and gathered them. Stone materials for making flaked stone knives, scrapers, and projectile points were not so readily available. The nearest source for these materials was in the Hat Creek Valley, located 20 km away as the crow flies, over the Clear Range mountains where people went during the summer and fall to hunt (see Figures 1.2, 2.5). Here, there were some deposits of cherts, but primarily there were deposits of very fine, almost glassy, black, igneous rocks known as trachydacites. This type of material occurred as nodules up to 30 cm long in the highland streambeds. It seems certain that some of this material was worked in the mountains to obtain specialized shapes, such as roughed out versions of the bifacial knives (bifaces) used by hunters, and the long endscraper blanks used by women to work on hides (Figure 5.1). When people returned to Keatley Creek from their summer and fall hunting and plant gathering, they must have brought with them these specialized tool blanks. They would need these tools for winter work and spring food-gathering activities. It is also clear that people brought along other cobbles of unworked stone, or cores, to make small flake tools whenever they were required to cut or scrape something during the winter or spring. We find exhausted cores and considerable amounts of flaking debris in the housepits at Keatley Creek. Tools made from the cores seem to have been made "expediently," or as needed. They were generally small, with some evidence of light resharpening, and often discarded after a short period of use. Larger flakes with longer use potential were sometimes stored against the walls.

The amount of stone available for performing tasks at the pithouses such as scraping hides, making bows and arrows, baskets, clothing, nets and fishing gear,

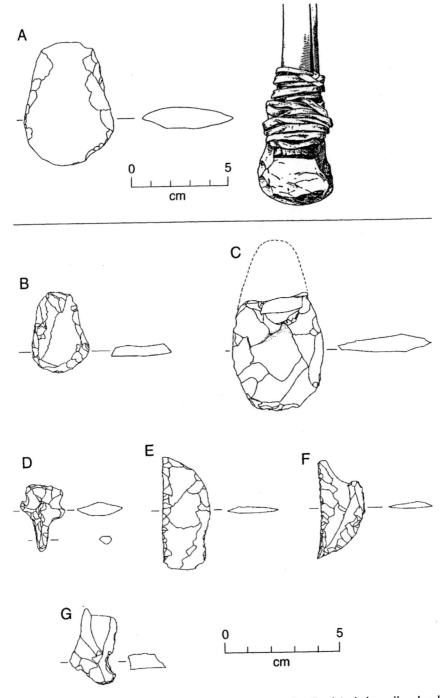

FIGURE 5.1. *Some of the stone artifact types present at Keatley Creek include spall and end scrapers used by women for working hides (A, B), bifaces used as knives by hunters while on long forays (C), drills (D), expedient pressure-retouched knives (E, F), and notches (G).*

and various ornaments was limited because of the 20 km distance from the mountain stone sources. In the winter, no more stone for tools could be obtained from the distant, snow-covered and frozen sources. The small size of most tools may have been one way of economically using the cores that were brought to the site; and the expedient manufacture of these tools as needed probably was one way of using only what was necessary from the cores for the infrequent and uncertain manufacturing activities carried out in the houses. Bifaces were also resharpened or finished, and other tools such as drills, hidescrapers, and arrowheads or spearheads were made in the pithouses. These tools were kept and resharpened over long periods of time until they broke or wore out. Much of the small flaking debris became incorporated in the floor deposits. Because of the dusty nature of the floor sediments, a number of smaller tools seem to have been lost or covered with dust and forgotten, including several unbroken arrowheads. When large chipping debris became too dense or cumbersome, it was undoubtedly collected and dumped on the roof or rim.

Other materials such as nephrite, ochre, and obsidian also required special trips to procure, or else had to be obtained via exchange with other groups. Because these items are so infrequent in the overall artifact assemblage, I will not deal with them in detail.

BASIC DISTRIBUTIONS

The recording of artifacts in terms of small subsquares only 50 cm on a side adds a great deal of paperwork and analysis to archaeological projects. However, if spatial distributions are important for research goals, this is one of the best and most efficient ways of recording the necessary information. Being able to determine the spatial distributions of artifacts across the floors of housepits was very important for the FRICGA project since this information could tell us what happened, where it happened within the housepits, and how people arranged themselves both socially and economically within their dwellings.

Fire-cracked rocks

As an example of what basic distributions can tell archaeologists, let us examine the lowly, often denigrated and ignored, fire-crack rock. This is a class of relatively ordinary rocks that have been heated in a fire. In a housepit, these rocks were commonly placed in birch bark containers with water, dried roots, berries, and fish to make soups. The hot rocks quickly made the water boil. Outside the pithouses, rocks could be heated for use in roasting pits, sweat baths, and a variety of other minor activities requiring heat. After being heated and suddenly cooled by placing them in water a number of times, the rocks cracked and broke apart. When they became too small to use they were discarded and new ones took their place.

What could the distribution of fire-cracked rocks tell us about activities or social organization in housepits? Jim Spafford undertook an analysis and found out three very important things. First, as already noted in the discussion of roof formation processes, the analysis of fire-cracked rocks in the roof showed there were particular parts of the roof where people threw refuse that might be bothersome, especially bits of sharp-edged fire-cracked rock (see Figure 3.9). Presumably, these were areas of the roof that were not used or walked upon very much; they also correspond to the northeast part of the roof that has the least amount of winter sun.

Second, the distribution of fire-cracked rocks across the floor of the largest house-pit (HP 7) revealed a number of very distinct areas of dense rock deposits (Figure 5.2). What could this reveal about the fundamental divisions of space in this housepit, especially about the activity versus family divisions within the house? Melena Nastich, one of the few ethnographers of the Lillooet, recorded bits of Lillooet oral history. One of these selections, quoted in chapter 2, recounted how each family had its own pile of cooking rocks in the traditional houses. If you examine Figure 5.2 carefully, you will see there is a strong tendency for each dense cluster of fire-cracked rocks to be associated with a fire-reddened, or hearth, area. This is true of both the left and the right sides of the house although the largest clusters, like the largest hearths, tend to occur on the left side of the house. This is one indication that both sides of the house were occupied by a number of separate families, where the same types of activities took place, although perhaps not with the same intensity.

The third important piece of information the fire-cracked rocks provided was that there were clear distributions, not to mention clear associations, with hearth areas. This fact demonstrated that far from being churned and mixed beyond recognition, the sediments we had identified in the field as "floor" versus roof sediments were relatively uncontaminated, intact, floor deposits. If everything had been mixed-up, as some people had suggested, then the distributions of fire-cracked rock across what we thought were floors should have resembled the distribution of fire-cracked rock on the roofs (refer to Figure 3.9). There would have been no way that they could have become so closely associated with the separate hearth areas across the floor of Housepit 7. Thus, the distribution of fire-cracked rocks provided an important proof demonstrating that we had recovered relatively intact, uncontaminated living floors. When we first saw the full distribution of fire-cracked rocks across the Housepit 7 floor, the entire team of analysts breathed a great sigh of relief after many years of working on faith and preliminary indications. This observation meant that other patterns of tools, bones, and plants should also be meaningful.

Of course, the occurrence of fire-cracked rocks also indicated that people were cooking foods in these houses on a relatively regular, but by no means daily basis. The total fire-cracked rock from the entirety of Housepit 7 amounted to only about 1,300 fragmented floor pieces and 12,500 roof pieces. If the floor deposits accumulated over 20 years, this would only amount to 65 fragments of cooking rocks being used per year (and far fewer whole rocks) for the entire house. This is quite low given the high rate of breakage of these rocks. Usually, rocks can be used only about four to five times before breaking up. In the smaller houses, there are much smaller amounts of fire-cracked rocks, often clustered in one corner of the house, indicating even less frequent use.

Chips and tools

If each hearth in the house, whether on the left side or the right side, were the focal point of a domestic group such as a nuclear or extended family, then, like the repeated

Housepit 7—Fire-Cracked Rock

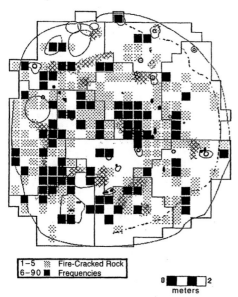

1-5 ▨	Fire-Cracked Rock
6-90 ■	Frequencies

0 ■■■■ 2
meters

Housepit 7—Debitage

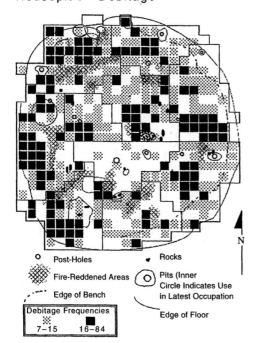

N

o	Post-Holes	•	Rocks
▨	Fire-Reddened Areas	⊙	Pits (Inner Circle Indicates Use in Latest Occupation)
⸴‑‑‑	Edge of Bench		

Debitage Frequencies
▨   ■
7-15   16-84

⌒ Edge of Floor

FIGURE 5.2. *Top: The distribution of fire-cracked rocks across the floor of Housepit 7 clearly shows that these rocks cluster adjacent to heavily fire-reddened areas. Other minor concentrations may represent little used areas where broken rocks may have been placed for storage or provisional discard. As in other distribution maps, the straight lines on the floors indicate the division of the floor into "sectors" for the purposes of analysis. Sectors were determined by the location of hearths, major postholes, storage pits, and the clustering of artifacts. Bottom: The distribution of debitage on the floor of Housepit 7. Note that debitage clusters around hearths, especially in areas between the hearths and house wall, while fire-cracked rocks tend to concentrate on the opposite side of the hearths near the center of the house. There are two substantial clusters in the center of the floor near lightly fire-reddened areas that may represent domestic areas of people occupying the north half of the center of the floor. Both figures are from Spafford (1991).*

clusters of fire-cracked rocks associated with each hearth, there should also be other common tools and objects that each family would have needed and used. Probably the most common objects made and used by all families were stone tools and debitage debris that resulted from their manufacture. Jim Spafford (1991) examined the

Housepit 7

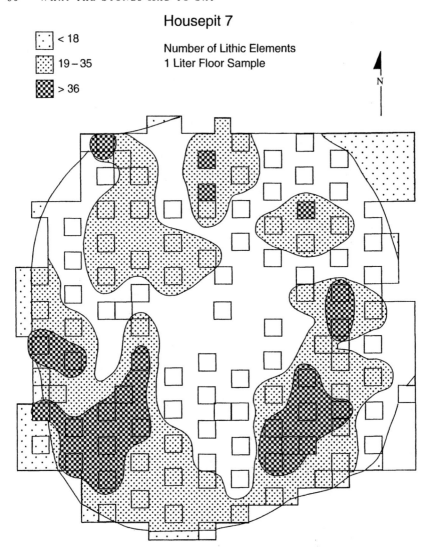

Number of Lithic Elements
1 Liter Floor Sample

FIGURE 5.3. *The distribution of "mesodebitage" (flakes of stone between 1–10 mm in size) across the floor of Housepit 7. Such small waste material is generally thought to accumulate at the actual places where stone reduction took place. Note that the high densities of these materials correspond quite closely to the dense areas of large debitage in Figure 5.2, indicating that normal debitage concentrations reflect stone working activities rather than storage or cleanup activities.*

distribution of stone debitage on the floor and found a striking set of dense, stone artifact clusters associated with each hearth (see Figure 5.2). This strongly suggests that each of the two sides of the house were occupied by several distinct domestic groups, rather than people performing different activities on the left and right sides of the house. Moreover, there is a clear pattern of the debitage occurring mainly between the hearth and the adjacent wall (except for the hearth in the center of the floor), which may indicate that people who made stone tools did so in the comfort and warmth of their sleeping areas. This again strongly reinforces the conclusion that the floor deposits were intact.

Because pieces of waste like debitage are often viewed as encumbrances or dangerous for people walking barefooted, and because waste tends to accumulate in unacceptable amounts in any location inhabited for more than a few weeks, people inhabiting sites for long periods of time typically engage in housecleaning activities. People periodically gather up all waste larger than a few centimeters and place it in a special area or container for later disposal, or they throw it out directly. This is called *secondary refuse* since it does not occur where it was produced. Some objects slated for discard may also be placed in special areas on the chance that they might be useful someday. Studies by Michael Schiffer (1987) and Knut Fladmark (1982) have shown that while larger pieces of refuse are regularly removed from living areas, the small bits of waste that are produced where people work are rarely removed. They are simply too small to pick up and discard. On the sand and gravel floors of the Keatley Creek housepits, small fragments would have certainly been left behind.

Therefore, we took soil samples at regular intervals from the floors to determine whether the concentrations of debitage we recovered from our screens really represented the locations where people made stone tools, or whether the concentrations of debitage simply represented accumulations of secondary refuse from cleaning up the floors. Figure 5.3 clearly shows that the small bits of flaked stone correspond almost exactly with the location of the major debitage concentrations. Since most of this debitage is also relatively small (average size is about 2 cm), it, too, seems to have been considered not worth the effort of removing.

Jim Spafford also found that the distribution of all modified stone tools (rather than just the debitage waste), displayed exactly the same cluster pattern around hearths as the debitage, and has the same implications. In addition, when the specific types of tools surrounding each hearth are compared, about 50% of them are the same types and occur in the same proportions; that is, each hearth has *at least* 1% arrowheads, 8% expedient knives, 9% scrapers, 17% utilized flakes, and so forth (Figure 5.4). This same basic pattern, or tool kit, also occurs in the other houses we excavated. Given the limited numbers of tools associated with some of the hearths (40 to 50 tools), and given variations between individuals or families in aptitudes for different activities, the tools associated with each hearth are very similar to those at the other hearths. Whenever individual artifacts are affected by randomizing factors such as how often specific activities take place, haphazard cleanup of debris, and displacement by foot traffic, then large numbers of artifacts are needed to accurately gauge the average overall assemblage composition of a group. Usually, archaeologists like to have 100 or more artifacts for a representative sample.

There are no indications that some tools were used more on the right side of the house than on the left, or vice versa (Figure 5.4). This also strongly reinforces the notion that hearths on the left and right sides of the house were focal points for a number of domestic groups or families rather than areas for different activities. Only a curious lack of debitage in the southernmost sector of the house and the central floor in front of this sector seem anomalous. But we shall return to this anomaly shortly.

Finally, granite boulders or cobbles that were found resting on the floor were probably used as anvils for breaking up bones and for similar activities. It is

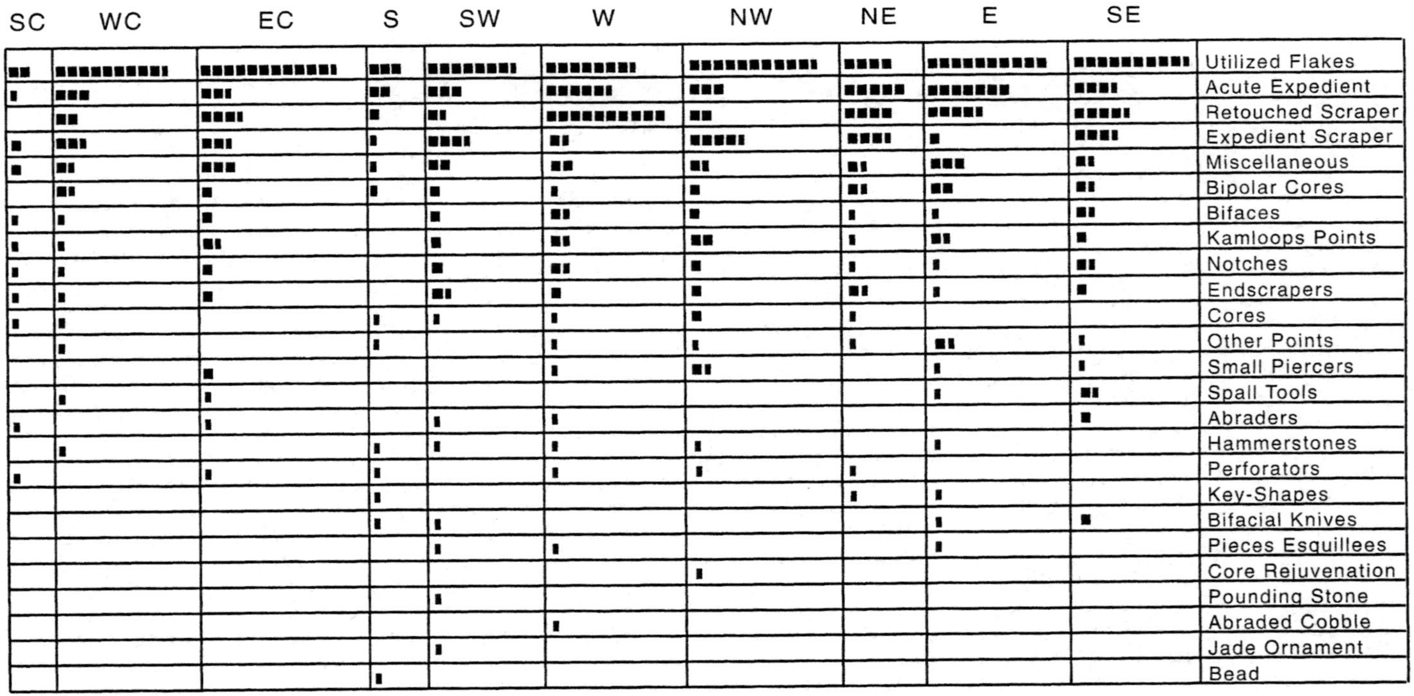

FIGURE 5.4. This chart represents the number of specific artifact types that occurred in each sector of the floor of Housepit 7. Note the general similarity between all of the sectors with the exception of the unusually low counts of modified tools in the south and south central sectors. Each complete point (■) represents three artifacts; partial points represent one or two artifacts. From Spafford (1991).

interesting that these boulders occur almost systematically between two hearths (or at least near a hearth) all the way around the interior of the house. The largest of these boulders occur in the left side of the house, once again indicating the presence of families at all the hearths, and perhaps more bone breaking occurred in this area. Abrading stones were also present around each hearth within the house.

ACTIVITY AREAS

If all the evident clusters seem to indicate there were a number of separate domestic units or families associated with the separate hearths in the housepit, what about activity areas? Are there no indications of special areas for different activities such that men and women might perform? If you carefully compare the top and bottom of Figure 5.2, you will notice that the clusters of fire-cracked rock have a strong tendency to occur on the side of the hearths toward the center of the floor, whereas the clusters of debitage occur on the opposite side of the hearths toward the house walls. Large biface fragments are associated with the locations of the fire-cracked rocks (Figure 5.5); notches also tend to occur in the center of the floors; and arrowheads, together with heavily retouched scrapers, tend to occur near the walls (Figure 5.5).

What do these distributions mean? In a number of myths and tales that James Teit recorded, wives are described as handing their husbands food *across* the hearth. This would seem to indicate that women habitually occupied one side of a hearth during meals (probably where they prepared food), while men occupied the other side of the hearth. The distribution of fire-cracked rocks versus the densest occurrences of debitage certainly seems to imply some such division of space. However, the situation is probably more complex since large bifaces are generally thought to be part of men's long-distance hunting tool kits, yet the fragments occur in the same general areas as the fire-cracked rocks that women used, although the flakes from resharpening these bifaces are found in the sleeping areas near the walls. It is possible that the parts of domestic areas closest to the center of the house were simply used for activities that tended to be dirty or messy such as cooking, butchering, hide working, or removing bark from arrow shafts, bow staves, spears, handles, or other wood objects.

In contrast, the heavily retouched scrapers near the walls probably represent storage locations of commonly used items that had little value since most of them were left when the house was abandoned. Heavily retouched or resharpened tools that were near the end of their use-lives may have been provisionally discarded under sleeping platforms along the walls. The occurrence of whole arrowheads in the same areas near the walls probably represents items lost during storage or during manufacturing. Considerable manufacturing must have taken place between the hearths and walls given all the stone debris found in these areas.

This pattern of some types of tools being concentrated between the hearth and the wall, while other types of tools are concentrated between the hearth and the center of the house is relatively strong and involves other kinds of tools, such as utilized flakes and notches. However, this pattern breaks down in one area of the house (Figure 5.6). This is the southern sector, the part of the central floor immediately in front of it that was previously mentioned. Not only does little debitage occur in this area, but also there are few examples of any other stone tool types. The few

Housepit 7 – Biface Fragments

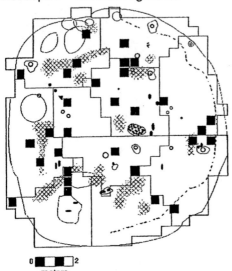

0 ▮▮▮▯ 2
meters

Housepit 7 – Heavily Retouched Scrapers

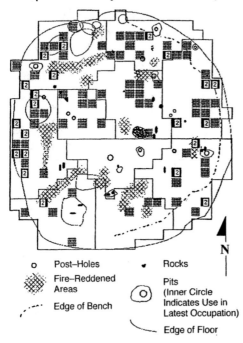

○   Post–Holes   ✦ Rocks

▨   Fire–Reddened
     Areas   ◎ Pits
                           (Inner Circle
⌁⌁   Edge of Bench   Indicates Use in
                           Latest Occupation)

                        ⌣ Edge of Floor

N

FIGURE 5.5. *Top: The distribution of biface fragments and bifaces on the floor of Housepit 7 showing their strong tendency to occur between the hearths and the center of the house.*
Bottom: The distribution of heavily retouched scrapers on the floor of Housepit 7 showing their strong tendency to cluster between the hearths and the wall of the house in a fashion that is complementary to the distribution of bifaces and some other artifact types. The location of these scrapers may represent storage or provisional discard behavior. Both figures are from Spafford (1991).

that do occur there conform to the basic types found around the other hearths. In this southern sector, we have large developed hearths, we have storage pits, we have diminished amounts of stone materials, but with the same characteristics as the other hearths. The spatial separation of stone tool use also breaks down here. What was going on at this location? Was it vacant most of the time? Was it a side entrance area? Was it a sacred area? Or is it possible that it was the residential location of the most

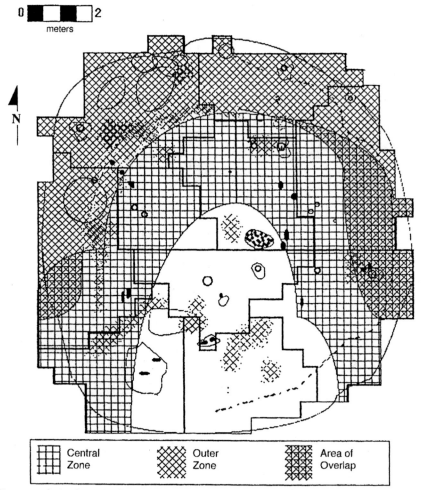

FIGURE 5.6. *A schematic illustration of the basic division of the floor of Housepit 7 into general activity areas near the wall versus near the floor center. This division is based on tool distributions such as those in Figures 5.2 and 5.5 as well as others. Of special note is the breakdown of this division of activity areas in the southern and south central sectors (without any shading), which may have been special residential, sacred, or traffic sectors. From Spafford (1991).*

important family in the house—the house "chief" or administrative head? There are ample observations from the Northwest Coast native communities that the chiefs did little physical work. Most of their time was spent arranging loans, feasts, marriages, funerals, and displaying the wealth and success of the house by *not* performing physical work. It is perhaps not just a coincidence that the only nephrite fragment found in Housepit 7, and perhaps an ornamental one at that, came from a pit in the south sector. While it may be premature to determine exactly why this southern sector is so unusual, we at least have some very good leads. Future excavations of large houses should help to resolve this question.

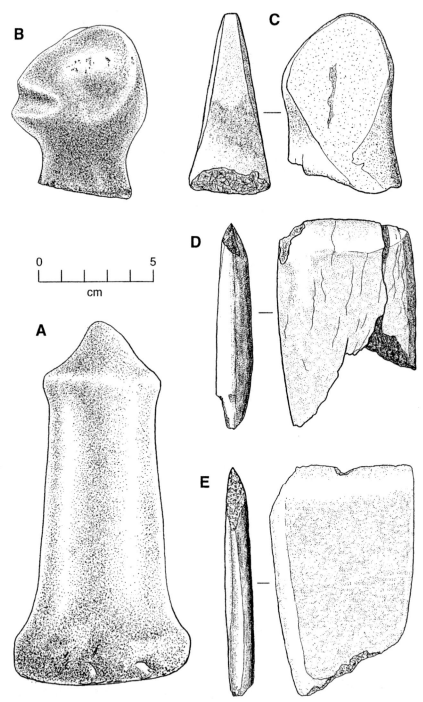

FIGURE 5.7A. *Some of the prestige stone artifacts recovered from Keatley Creek included sculpted stone mauls (A, B), a unique piece of sculpted white marble that may have been the top of a maul (C), and nephrite adze blades (D, E).*

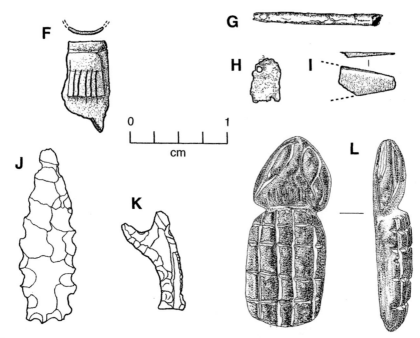

FIGURE 5.7B. *Additional prestige stone artifacts recovered from Keatley Creek included decorated steatite pipe bowl fragments (F), a copper tubular bead (G), a fragmentary copper sheet with a carefully made hole (H), the tip of a thin nephrite tool or ornament (I), a serrated chipped stone pendant (J), part of a chipped stone eccentric (K), and a small stone sculpture with a serpentlike head (L).*

PRESTIGE STONES

As noted at the outset of this chapter, there is a wide array of stone objects that can be considered prestige items. Most of these are unique or are represented only by two or three specimens. Examining the distribution of such objects is not very helpful, especially since virtually all of them were broken or lost and might have been kicked around, displaced by children playing, or possibly lost by visitors. Distributions are helpful only when there are large numbers of objects so that behavioral patterns can stand out from the random events that affect individual objects. Nevertheless, simply the presence of such prestige items, or their fragments, tells a great deal about the house and the community that owned or produced them.

For instance, nephrite is an attractive, green stone material that is very effective for cutting wood. It is almost indistinguishable from jade. It is also one of the toughest and hardest stones traditional societies ever attempted to use. Without industrial diamond-tipped saws, it takes about an hour to cut a groove in nephrite only 1–2 millimeters (mm) deep. There were many millimeters to cut in the manufacture of an adze blade (Figure 5.7). John Darwent (1996) estimates that at least 110 hours were required simply to cut out the adze blank. Many more hours were necessary to create the cutting edge and polish the surface. To cut nephrite, quartz sand was used with string or wood, the same technique used by the Chinese and Maoris to make their jade objects prior to the availability of industrial rock-cutting saws. The great amount of labor involved was one of the reasons jade and nephrite were so expensive in traditional societies. Nephrite was a sign of wealth, and it is entirely possible that much of the work done in the creation of nephrite objects was performed by slaves or servile members of the great houses. Some nephrite adzes were so long (45 cm) and narrow that they served exclusively as displays of wealth and status. A similar phenomenon is known for European Neolithic adzes. Simply the presence of nephrite objects indicates a great deal about the social and economic inequalities that must have existed at Keatley Creek and many other Plateau communities.

Copper, too, was rare and difficult to work. Prehistorically, no copper objects larger than a silver dollar are known. Copper also features as a rare element of wealth and wonder in some of the tales James Teit recorded. In one tale, it is associated with the sun. At Keatley Creek, we recovered several fragmentary sheets of copper and one rolled tubular bead about the size of a wooden matchstick which had obviously been lost in one of the storage pits in Housepit 7 (Figure 5.7). No other metal such as gold, silver, or iron has ever been recovered from a prehistoric context in the Northwest or Canada.

We also recovered intriguing fragments of what can only be termed chipped stone "eccentrics" (see Figure 5.7). These are objects of chert or trachydacite that were chipped into thin and unusual forms, often resembling the silhouettes of animals. Such objects occur elsewhere in the world and are something of an enigma since no one knows exactly how they were used or why they were made. However, in most cases where they occur, such as the Classic Maya, the Mississippian centers of the United States, and the predynastic Gerzean settlements of Egypt, they are associated with pronounced social and economic inequalities.

There are also tubular, soapstone pipe fragments, similar to modern-day chillums, which were probably used primarily by chiefs, shamans, and the elderly— if the ethnographies are any indication. It is possible many common people smoked wooden pipes (wooden pipes are mentioned by Strong, 1959, p. 139) and only the most wealthy people used stone pipes. There are also crude slate pendants and fragments of white sheet mica. There is a shaped piece of marble that resembles an animal head from a pestle. And there is a small, carved piece of serpentine that seems to have a snake's head (refer to Figure 5.7). At the neighboring Bell site, even more elaborate sculptures were found in the grave of a young child. All of these objects represent an unusual investment of time and energy in the procurement and manufacture of items for display. Their use was predominantly a social one. They were used to advertise the success, wealth, and desirability of belonging to the group that owned them. The message they conveyed to individuals outside the corporate group was "Come! Join us. We can offer you fine objects of art, jewelry, fine smoking, wealth, power, and good times." Thus, these objects tell us a great deal about the Keatley Creek community. The unusual effort involved in procuring or manufacturing these items makes sense only in a society where these objects were privately owned, or at least owned by families or corporate groups within the community. They have no real place in generalized hunter–gatherer communities where everything is shared. No one would put in all the hours of work and toil to make a nephrite adze only to have it "borrowed" by another community member, while the maker might never see it again. The person who put in all the effort to make such rare objects would receive no benefit for his work. The benefits would go to others. Labor-intensive prestige items make sense only where private property is recognized and where sharing is regulated.

SUMMARY

A great deal has been learned from simple stone tools. We could go into much greater detail in discussing the tool formation processes such as the procurement, the transport, the reduction and modifications, the sharpening techniques, and the discard of stone tools. But, for the present purposes, the most interesting results are found in examining the distributions of stone artifacts. These distributions clearly show that there were separate clusters of fire-cracked rocks, anvils, stone abraders, debitage, and tools associated with each hearth and storage pit in the largest house. Since these objects represent activities that were probably common to all families, the implication is that each hearth was occupied by a separate domestic group such as a family, extended family, or closely connected group of people. Each domestic area used by a "family" seems to have consisted of a sleeping, storage, tool-making zone between the hearth and the house wall, as well as a cooking-processing area on the other side of the hearth toward the center of the house floor. No clearly male versus female activity areas can be identified, although there are some probable female- and male-related activities. One zone of the living floor in the south stands out as different from the rest in terms of stone tool density and activity areas. This may have been the residence of the principal house administrator and titular head. Although we have excavated only one large housepit, I would predict that these patterns will be typical of other large housepits in the region.

The wide range of prestige lithic objects recovered from the site indicates the presence of substantial inequalities in wealth, as well as a very entrenched notion of private property at Keatley Creek.

CHAPTER 6

What the Plants Had to Say

Plant food constitutes the staff of life for many people throughout the world. In the Lillooet region, plants may not have held this importance since salmon was so central to the diet. But plants were still extremely important in traditional cultures for their vitamins, minerals, calories, and medicinal qualities. Plants were also critical for building shelters and making technological items essential in procuring salmon and other foods. Fibers and poles were necessary to create nets, while obtaining roots required digging sticks and plant matting for cooking in pits. Plants were also used to make life more comfortable and pleasurable in forms such as mats, dishes, clothing, bedding, and smoking. Thus, there is an entire technological realm in which plants were used.

What can be recovered from this great diversity of plant use at most archaeological sites? Many archaeologists never bother to ask the question, but simply assume that plants decay in the earth and that no remains have been preserved with the exception of charred pieces of wood left in hearths that can be radiocarbon dated. There are other problems with looking for prehistoric plant remains: removing and processing sediment samples increases excavation time and effort; the bags become heavy and cumbersome; finding someone to analyze them can be difficult; and devoting scarce excavation funds to search for plant remains may mean sacrificing other kinds of analysis for an enterprise with uncertain payoffs—or at least ones that are not immediately visible. Thus, few projects except those dealing with problems associated with the origin of agriculture systematically use plant recovery techniques in excavations.

At Keatley Creek, I thought there might be good reason to hope for some plant preservation. The region is semi-arid, which favors preservation; the insides of the housepits would have also provided a protected environment where plant materials might survive; and the use of fires for cooking would have also favored the charring of plant materials, thereby greatly increasing the likelihood of preservation. Contrary to what many people might expect, most archaeological sites actually have good potential for recovering and analyzing plant remains precisely because of this charring and preservation effect. This operates to preserve minute parts of plants such as seeds, just as charring preserves small pieces of wood. Archaeobotanists, also known as paleoethnobotanists, study the plant remains used at prehistoric sites. They generally use only charred materials in their analyses, thereby eliminating small plant parts that may have been introduced by natural agents such as mice, voles, and seeds falling through cracks, insect holes, or other spaces in the soil.

However, the rim deposits at Keatley Creek turned out to be extraordinarily dry microenvironments that preserved uncharred plant materials deposited as part of prehistoric housecleaning activities.

Thus, I planned to systematically sample the floors and the other deposits of housepits to see if there were important differences in the way plants were used across the floors, and from house to house. Sampling the roof and rims for botanical remains also helped to better understand their formation processes (see chapter 3). An added advantage of sampling the floor sediments was that it enabled us to look for small fragments of bone and stone to indicate precisely where activities took place. We also used such samples for chemical analysis of the soils. However at the beginning of the project, there was no assurance that we could successfully identify living floor deposits, much less extract botanical information that would be useful for determining social and economic organization within housepits. I was encouraged by Dana Lepofsky, who was present on my first field crew. She was a specialist studying prehistoric plant remains and went on to analyze the many thousands of plant remains we recovered from the site.

BOTANICAL FORMATION PROCESSES

Ethnographically, pithouses were used only in the wintertime, and in fact, the entire *raison d'être* of pithouses makes sense only in terms of winter conditions. According to Teit, people were anxious to get out of the crowded pithouses in the spring. We have found no archaeological indication they were used in the summertime when camping under shade trees would have been more pleasant. The only plants that would have been available for use during the winter in the immediate surroundings of Keatley Creek were firewood, conifer branches for bedding, small cactus leaves, and any dried berries such as rosehips that still remained on the bushes. Based on knowledge of the geographical distribution and seasonality of plants recovered at Keatley Creek, we can conclude that the vast majority of plant food remains recovered at the site probably were transported there during the summer in a dried state from distant locations such as the mountains or the river terraces. In the late fall, just prior to occupying the pithouses for the winter, many technological materials were probably also brought to the houses, including conifer branches, grass, and incidental plants used for bedding; materials for making mats and baskets such as reeds and birch bark; materials for repairing the pithouse roof (conifer needles, bark, poles); materials for making bows, arrows, string, rope, nets, hoops, and other objects; materials for making clothes and armor (sagebrush bark and birch bark), and firewood. Wastes from many of these materials were probably thrown out onto the rim in an uncharred state; occasionally some of these items became charred and the smaller bits became incorporated into the floor sediments where we recovered them.

DISTRIBUTIONS ACROSS THE FLOOR

The most striking pattern of botanical remains Dana Lepofsky found in the housepit floors was a concentration of Douglas fir and pine needles, grass seeds, and

Housepit 7

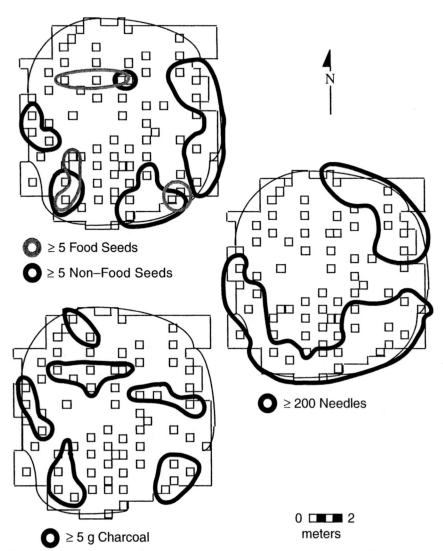

○ ≥ 5 Food Seeds

● ≥ 5 Non–Food Seeds

● ≥ 200 Needles

● ≥ 5 g Charcoal

0 ▭▮▮▮ 2
meters

FIGURE 6.1. *Distributions of charred food seeds, non-food seeds, conifer needles, and char-coal across the living floor of Housepit 7. Non-food seeds are primarily composed of chenopod and grass seeds that were included together with pine and Douglas fir boughs as part of the bedding used near the walls of the house. These results clearly show that both the right and the left sides of the house were used for sleeping. The restricted occurrence of food seeds seems to indicate special preparation and storage areas for some plant foods. The small squares in these diagrams represent the sampled squares upon which these distri-butions are based. From Lepofsky et al. (1995).*

chenopod seeds around the edge of the floors near the rims (Figure 6.1). Some of this made a great deal of sense on the basis of ethnographic analogy, for Teit recorded the traditional sleeping areas as being against the walls either on mats or on elevated benches, as well as the use of Douglas fir boughs and grass for bedding. Many dried needles and grass seeds from this bedding must have fallen to the floor only to become carbonized or completely consumed by fire when the housepit roof was burned. However, the occurrence of chenopod seeds was unexpected since no mention of this plant is made ethnographically either as a food or as a material used for other purposes. Yet, its distribution largely coincided with the fir needles and grass seeds and constitutes the single most common type of seed remain found in the housepits. At this point, it seems this common weed may simply have been obtained as an incidental plant growing among the grass gathered for bedding.

The strong pattern of charred conifer needles near the walls of the houses makes a great deal of logical and ethnographic sense. More important, it demonstrates once again that the floor deposits identified in the field were not simply mixed deposits—which could never be used to infer activities or social organization within the houses. The concentrations of the needles clearly indicated where the sleeping areas were located within the houses. More importantly, in the case of the largest housepit we excavated (HP 7), the needles demonstrated that these sleeping areas extended almost all the way around the floor. This in turn, reinforced the conclusion that *both* sides of the house were used by families as domestic areas where people slept, cooked, ate, and performed other common domestic tasks.

An analysis by William Middleton of enriched chemical elements in the soils of the floors produced similar patterns to those of the plant materials and points to an essentially identical conclusion. For instance, phosphorous, potassium, calcium, and magnesium often become concentrated in areas where people have lived because decaying plant and animal materials, ash from fires, as well as human wastes, impregnate the soils with these elements, all of which are relatively insoluble and remain at locations where they are deposited. The distribution of some of these elements (potassium, phosphorous) on the floor of Housepit 7 probably reflects eating activities or the spread of wood ash around hearth areas (Figure 6.2). Other elements such as magnesium and calcium are more concentrated around single hearths and may represent specialized activity wastes, such as the breaking up of bones or the discard of small bones from soups or fish (Figure 6.2). It is important to note that these element concentrations show no indication of different activities having been performed on the right versus the left side of the house. The concentrations of these elements are associated with hearth and perimeter areas on both sides of the house, indicating that food processing and consumption took place on both sides of the house. In fact, the concentrations of chemicals match the concentrations of small bone fragments almost exactly (refer to Figure 7.3). Patterns where one side of a house is used for special activities do occur, however, in some of the smaller housepits, such as Housepit 9 (Figure 6.3), which reflects a very different kind of social and economic organization.

There are few indications of plant-processing activity areas in the large house. One might have expected plants to be cooked and used, and some bits accidentally charred, around every hearth. But the only real concentration of food plant seeds occurs in the north central sector of the house with more minor occurrences near a hearth in the southwest part of the floor, and near a probable storage location close to the wall (see Figure 6.1). Whether this is because one or two domestic groups

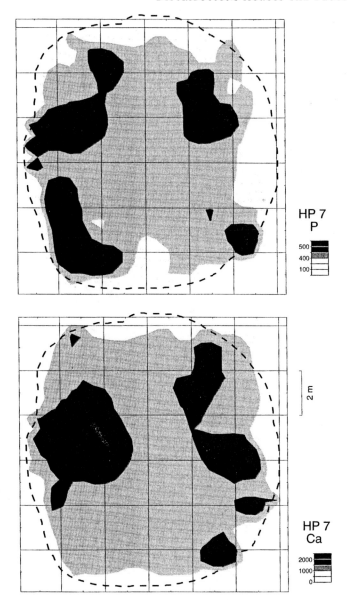

FIGURE 6.2. *Concentrations of phosphorous (top) and calcium (bottom) in the floor sediments of Housepit 7 as determined by William Middleton. Phosphorous becomes concentrated due to food wastes and ash being incorporated into the soils, while calcium becomes concentrated due to bone fragments and other calcium-rich materials becoming incorporated into the floor. Note, again, similar concentrations on both sides of the house associated with food preparation areas around hearths and eating areas near the walls. These distributions are based on the same soil samples as the botanical distributions.*

collected and used more plants, or because one person was an herbalist for the entire house, or because only one family prepared special plant foods used in feasts, or

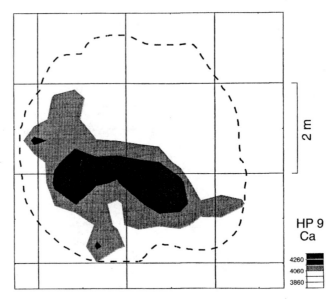

FIGURE 6.3. *In contrast to the symmetrical distribution of waste-related chemical elements on both sides of the Housepit 7 floor as seen in Figure 6.2, William Middleton found that small houses exhibit a very different organization indicating that only a single activity area was present for processing and probably consuming food as is evident in the distribution of calcium across the floor of Housepit 9, shown here. These distributions indicate a much more communally oriented house organization than the segmented and hierarchical domestic areas of the large housepit.*

because all the women gathered at one location to prepare their plant foods cannot be determined at this point. Some sort of specialized activity area, if not specialization, is definitely indicated by these remains. The size of the largest seed-related activity area and the small total number of seeds involved are both indicative of the work area of a single, occasionally active, individual specialist, rather than a large group of women working communally. A similar specialized concentration of food and non-food seeds occurred on the floor of the medium-sized housepit we excavated.

SUBSISTENCE

Food plant remains are remarkably scarce in the housepits we excavated, including the rims. This may simply be a matter of careful and almost complete consumption on the parts of inhabitants, but typically, small children are careless with food, and it would seem likely that occasional amounts would have been spilled near the fires and charred. The rarity of charred food remains may also be due to the infrequent use of fires within the housepits (see chapter 4). The rarity of food remains might also be due to dogs consuming food that fell to the ground, except that dogs do not appear to have been kept inside housepits ethnographically (Teit, 1917, p. 46; 1912a, pp. 250, 256, 307; 1912b, p. 325), and almost none of the bones on housepit floors exhibit gnaw marks from dogs. Some food remains, such as the lilies and mountain potatoes, may not be represented archaeologically simply because their starch-like bulbs and corms do not preserve very well. Moreover, these root foods, like most other plants, were generally precooked or processed elsewhere, thus leaving fewer remains at winter pithouse villages. The rarity of food remains may also have been due to a limited amount of consumption of stored plant foods during the winter. It would have been very difficult to transport any large quantities of plant foods from the mountains to the village at Keatley Creek, especially since valuable dried deer meat, hides, and flaking stone needed to be transported as well. On the other hand, the sources of Saskatoon berries (service berries), kinnikinnik berries, and rose hips would have been much closer, and these are the most commonly occurring charred food remains recovered at Keatley Creek (Table 6.1). Few of the food remains can be attributed to the summer mountain food-gathering areas. At this point, there is no compelling reason to expect that large quantities of berries and bulbs were being eaten during the winter. I would estimate the total amount of these foods brought down from the high mountains to be about half of the total amount gathered there, or about 20–40 kg per family, especially since women had to carry the family foods, belongings, and camping gear when traveling (Teit, 1917, p. 37). The same amount of onions and berries from the river terraces might have been stored for the winter (see Turner, 1992). The high number of plant taxa in the houses indicates that there was a substantial use of plants, but processing and preservation biases may have limited the absolute number of food plants recovered archaeologically.

TECHNOLOGY

It is in the technological domain where plant remains are the most abundant. In addition to the major structural elements used in the construction of the house roofs (chapter 4), and the bedding materials already noted, there were many pieces of charcoal scattered throughout all types of housepit deposits. Most of this charcoal undoubtedly came from the burning of wood in hearths. Analysis of this charcoal clearly showed that people were using the pine and Douglas fir wood from the mountain slopes behind the site for firewood. They were not using many of the cottonwood or other deciduous trees from the creek bed.

However, there was a surprise in some of the housepits. In a medium-sized housepit (HP 3), we encountered a row of carbonized boards, about 15 cm wide and one cm thick, arranged at the foot of one wall. Although I had known that James Teit reported benches along the walls for sleeping, I had not expected to find actual boards preserved in the houses. A small section of plank was also recovered from the central area of Housepit 7. Surprisingly, these boards were made of cottonwood, a fairly soft wood, and perhaps the easiest to split with antler wedges and stone celts.

I had hoped to find parts of burned, wooden tools among the charred remains of the floor or in the rim deposits; however, people seem to have been conscientious about burning any available pieces of wood in their hearths. In the entire site, we recovered only a single piece of charred, worked wood. In Housepit 90, a small housepit, there was a segment that appears to have been part of a bow stave or a hoop for a fishing net.

Table 6.1
Archaeobotanical Remains Recovered From the Floor
of Three Housepits at Keatley Creek*

Scientific Name (Common Name)	Part Found†	Frequency			Primary Use‡
		Large HP (HP 7)	Medium HP (HP 3)	Small HP (HP 12)	
Acer cf. glabrum (maple)	C	1			T
Alnus cf. sinuata (alder)	C	1			T
Amelanchier alnifolia (saskatoon)	S	40	27	2	F
Arcostaphylos uvaursi (kinnikinnik)	S	9	11		F
Artemesia tridentata (big sagebrush)	C	1			T
Betula papyrifera (paper birch)	C	1			T
? Boraginaceae (Borage Family)	S	1			?
Carex sp. (sedge)	S		1		T
Chenopodium sp. (chenopod)**	S	148	36	10	?
Cornus sericea (red-osier dogwood)	S	3			F
Ericaceae (Heather Family)	S	62	44	2	? F
Graminae (grass) **	S	77	9		T
——	O	79	115		T
Juniperus sp. (juniper)	C	1			T
Opuntia sp. (prickly pear)	S	2	12		F
Phacelia sp.	S	20	7		O

I also hoped to find remains of basketry since baskets and birch bark containers were extensively used in the historic period. We did find innumerable pieces of birch bark in all types of deposits, but only a few of these had puncture holes where seams had been sewn together. Birch bark was also apparently used for many other things from lining storage pits, to lighting fires, to wrapping up small items for storage, to birch bark armor (Teit, 1912a, pp. 244, 340; 1912b, p. 319). Therefore, much of the birch bark we recovered may simply represent scraps from manufacturing or remains from other items. We found not a single piece of coiled and decorated basketry that

TABLE 6.1 (CONTINUED)
ARCHAEOBOTANICAL REMAINS RECOVERED FROM THE FLOOR
OF THREE HOUSEPITS AT KEATLEY CREEK*

Scientific Name (Common Name)	Part Found[†]	Frequency			Primary Use[‡]
		Large HP (HP 7)	Medium HP (HP 3)	Small HP (HP 12)	
Pinus ponderosa (ponderosa pine)	N	10078	7521		T
——	C	64	27		T
Populus sp. (cottonwood)	C	1	2		T
Prunus sp. (cherry)	S	4			F
Psuedotsuga menziesii (Douglas fir)	N	18129	835		T
——	C	219	87		T
——	S		5		?
Rosa cf. *woodsii* (rose)	S	9	1		F
Scirpus sp. (rush)	S	1			T
Silene sp.	S		1		O
Smilacina stellata (solomon's seal)		2			F
Ribes cf. *inerme* (gooseberry)	S				F
Unidentified	C	62	24		—
Unidentified	S	94	16	2	—
Total N[††]	C	350	140	—	—
Total N	S	474	172	16	—

*Note.**Miscellaneous plant parts, such as buds, bark, and other plant tissues are not included here. See Lepofsky, 1993a, for complete presentation of data.
[†]C = charcoal; S = seed; N = needle; O = other
[‡]F = food; T = technology; O = other; see Lepofsky, 1993a, for more detailed ethnobotanical descriptions.
**There is no ethnobotanical or paleoethnobotanical evidence that either chenopods or grass seeds were ever eaten in the Interior Plateau.
[††] Charcoal from only a small number of the total flotation samples were identified. No charcoal specimens from HP 12 were identified. From Lepofsky et al., 1995.

the historical Stl'alt'imx were renowned for manufacturing.[1] Birch bark containers were easier to manufacture and may have been more watertight. For this reason, they may have been more commonly used by most people. If coiled basketry existed in the Interior Plateau 1,000 years ago, it may have been owned and used exclusively by the

[1] In the 1996 field season, as this book was going to press, one piece of burned coiled basketry was found on the floor of a structure that I suspect was used for ritual feasting. The structure has only been partially excavated, however, and we have not yet dated its occupation.

wealthiest households and used only for special occasions, such as feasting, just as the best dinnerware in modern households is brought out only for special meals. Because of their great value, coiled baskets may have been highly curated and used as grave goods in high status burials, leaving little trace of their existence in housepits. Their great value would also explain why so many were produced and sold to white colonizers. Even today, these coiled baskets sell for many hundreds of dollars.

SMOKING

About 1,200 years ago, stone pipes began to be left in archaeological deposits on the Plateau, and we recovered a number of stone pipe fragments at Keatley Creek. There is some debate as to exactly what people were smoking in these pipes. By the time the first ethnographers made their observations, tobacco was in use, but was it introduced by the fur trade or had it been present long before that time? If tobacco was smoked in prehistoric communities, it would constitute the best case for the use of a domesticated plant on the Plateau.

We observed charred residues adhering to the inside of pipe fragments just as charred crusts and residues build up in modern pipes. I submitted the prehistoric pipe fragments with residues for analysis to Wayne Jeffery, the head of the toxicology section of the Royal Canadian Mounted Police in Vancouver and to Dr. B. M. Kapur, the Director of Laboratories at the Addiction Research Foundation in Toronto. Both of these analysts used gas chromatography–mass spectrometry to investigate the residues. Although their results disclosed abundant organic compounds present in the pipe residues—while other stones from the same matrix showed almost *no* organic remains—none of the organic compounds corresponded to nicotine or any distinctive nicotine breakdown products. No alkaloids of any sort were present. Thus, it seems entirely possible that prehistorically, smoking on the Plateau involved the use of other substances such as kinnikinick, Indian lovage, and dogbane, plants that are still smoked in the region. Documenting smoking at the Keatley Creek site is important, since, ethnographically, smoking seems to have been confined to important people of the community, such as elites, shamans, and elders. Unfortunately, we did not recover any of the pipe fragments from floor contexts; they were all found in roof deposits, apparently discarded after they had broken.

SUMMARY

Although plant remains are often ignored because they are so difficult to see and recover without special techniques, they provide invaluable information on the social and economic life of prehistoric dwellers of pithouses. They reveal not only what plant foods were eaten inside the pithouses, but also reflect transportation constraints, technology, seasonality, and other factors. The relative diversity of plant remains in various houses demonstrates that occupants of smaller houses used a far narrower range of plants than occupants of larger houses.

In the small house we investigated, there were fewer plant remains in the floor deposits, only 16 seeds compared to hundreds from the larger house floors. There is no indication of any specialized plant-processing area in the small houses. Moreover, statistical analyses showed that the greater diversity of plant remains in the large house was due to more than increased sample size (Lepofsky et al., 1995). This seems to indicate that the occupants of smaller housepits differed significantly from the occupants of the larger houses in their use of plant materials. Economically, the occupants of the smaller housepits do not seem to have been as active or industrious in their use of plants.

The distribution of the remains of bedding materials indicates that people slept around most of the perimeter of the larger houses. This reinforces the conclusions from other analyses that domestic groups occupied both sides of the house and that differences between the two sides of the house are due to social and economic factors rather than the performance of different activities on the two sides of the house. Chemical elements associated with food wastes (phosphorous, calcium) also were concentrated near hearths and the wall on both sides of the house, confirming the basic conclusions from studying the plant remains.

Numerous remains of plants used for technological purposes (fire, house construction, bark basketry, planks) occur throughout the deposits and provide important insights into the nature of daily life. Evidence of some specialized areas for processing of plant foods in the larger houses, as well as evidence for smoking, provide more detailed glimpses into the past activities within the houses. The clear patterning in the distribution of plant remains and chemical elements across the floor deposits of the houses again demonstrates that we correctly distinguished floor deposits from roof deposits and that the floor deposits were relatively intact. They had not been hopelessly mixed with other sediments. If they had been, no patterning would have been apparent, and it certainly would not have concentrated Douglas fir and pine needles and grass seeds under the thickest parts of the overlying roof deposits, for those were the areas most deeply buried by the collapsing roof and therefore most protected from mixing.

CHAPTER 7

What the Bones Had to Say

Together with stones, bones constitute the meat and potatoes of most prehistoric archaeological analyses. Bones preserve relatively well, are generally easy to see and to recover during excavation, and clearly play key roles in the survival of prehistoric peoples over numerous generations. Many archaeologists are content with listing the species that are found at sites and indicating their relative importance, assuming that the economic importance of the remains speaks more or less for itself. However, when we begin examining the bone remains in detail, and try to understand the formation processes that are responsible for a particular assemblage, then things become more complex and less clear. If we try to probe the social and economic organization of past communities by looking at the bone remains, the quest becomes more involved. One topic where there is a lack of validated theories to link material remains to specific human behavior is the interpretation of faunal remains. However, let us see how far we can get. I will start with assemblage formation processes to establish a baseline of understanding.

FORMATION PROCESSES

I have already discussed some important contributions that the study of bones has made to our understanding of the formation processes of the floor and roof deposits (chapter 3). In that case, Karla Kusmer, who was the specialist analyzing the bone remains from Keatley Creek, found that bones had been exceptionally well-preserved in sediments identified as floor deposits, whereas bones were frequently weathered and fish bones were less numerous in the roof deposits. Now, it will be interesting to find out how those bones got to the site and what Kusmer's analyses revealed about past life at the site.

Two types of bone remains, salmon and deer, dominate the entire collection of bones collected at Keatley Creek (Table 7.1). Small numbers of mountain sheep, elk, dogs, beaver, hare, and bird bones occur, as well as some rarer species. To begin with, we will concentrate on salmon and deer since they are the two most important food species.

Salmon are born in inland freshwater streams and lakes. In their first year they migrate to the ocean where they feed and grow fat over the next few years. When they are ready to lay eggs, they gather together from vast reaches of the ocean in enormous schools and migrate up the rivers and streams to the places they were born. There, they spawn and die. Indians intercepted the salmon during these massive

Table 7.1
Faunal Remains Recovered From Three
Housepits Floors at Keatley Creek

Scientific Name (Common Name)	Frequency			Primary Use‡
	Large HP (HP 7)	Medium HP (HP 3)	Small HP (HP 12)	
Unidentified freshwater shellfish	5	2		T
Dentalium sp. (dentalium)	3			T
Hinnites giganteus (purple-hinged rock scallop)	1			T
Margaritifera falcata (freshwater shellfish)	2	—		T
Nucella sp. (dogwinkle)	1			T
Oncorhynchus sp. (salmon)	1344	314	31	F
Accipiter sp. (hawk)	2			T
Tetraonidae (grouse)	4			F
Bird		1		
Lepus americanus (snowshoe hare)	19			F, T
Castor canadensis (beaver)	16	4	3	F, T
Peromyscus sp. (deermouse)	1			
Microtus sp. (vole)	9			
Canis familiaris (domestic dog)	1	41 (MNI = 1)		
Vulpes vulpes (red fox)	1			T
Ursus arctos (grizzly)	1			T
Artiodactyl	27	12	3	F, T
Cervus elaphus (elk)			2	F, T
Odocoileus sp. (deer)	42	5	1	F, T
Ovis canadensis (bighorn sheep)	1			F, T
Unidentified large mammal	176	35	10	
Unidentified mammal	751	147	71	
Total NISP	2407	561	121	

Note. ‡ F = food; T = technology; see Kusmer, 1993a, for more detailed accounts of taxa.
From Lepofsky et al., 1995

migrations. Today, when salmon are caught by Indians in the Lillooet region, the heads, tails, fins, guts, and backbones are removed and thrown in the river or near the fish-processing structures by the river, sometimes forming huge piles in narrow ravines (Figure 7.1). In contrast, the nearby processing and drying areas, where literally thousands of fish are processed every year, remain virtually bone free. The resulting dried fillets are taken back to the villages bone free. However, these are modern practices and people apparently did things differently in the past for we do find fish bones in village sites.

We know from early ethnographic records that many bones were retained in more traditional butchering practices. A considerable amount of meat is always left on the backbones. Therefore, when food was scarce, the backbones—referred to humorously as "neckties"—were also dried and stored in bundles for use as snacks or in soups. The fins were frequently given to dogs (Albright, 1984, p. 63; Desmond Peters, personal

FIGURE 7.1. *Top: Salmon butchering and drying structures (seen from the air in Figure 2.3) where literally hundreds of salmon are butchered each season. Interestingly, not a single salmon bone can be found in or around most of these structures.*
Bottom: Instead, salmon remains are systematically removed from the butchering and drying areas and either dumped in nearby ravines, such as this one, or thrown back into the river. If archaeologists excavated only the butchering structures, they might never know that these areas were used for processing enormous amounts of salmon. In order to correctly infer the use of these areas, they would have to also excavate dumps such as this one, but these dumps occupy such a small area that finding them archaeologically would be like looking for a needle in a haystack.

communication). The oil-rich heads could be split and dried for winter soups, or boiled with other discarded parts to extract the precious oil that could keep people warm in the winter by producing calories and body heat. The smallest and least fat species of salmon, the pinks, were often simply dried without removing the backbone.

Given this butchering and processing scenario for salmon, what bones might be expected to end up at a winter village? There might be considerable numbers of pink salmon backbones, as well as bundles of sockeye and spring salmon backbones destined for snacks or soups. These bone bundles would probably have been placed at the bottom of the storage pits since they were of much less value compared to the dried fillets. If these backbones had been used in soups, then we might never have found them since cooking salmon bones softens them and makes them more susceptible to decay and disintegration, although we do not know precisely how much cooking is required for this to happen. Therefore, it is possible that none of the salmon bones found archaeologically were actually cooked. We require some detailed experiments to determine this possibility.

People may have gnawed off all the meat from the backbones and simply dropped the remaining bones on the floor where they would eventually separate and scatter. Archaeologically, we found these backbones were sometimes left, still articulated, in sleeping areas—probably remains of bedtime snacks. It seems likely that the vast majority of these discarded bones were gathered up and thrown on the roof periodically where dogs consumed most of them and the elements wore them down. We also found some bundles of bones left in the bottoms of pits, perhaps having gone rancid, or at least of such little value that they were not considered worth the effort of removing before the pit was filled in. Other less articulated bones may have broken off the bundles in removing them from the storage pits and fallen to the bottoms of the pits, or they may have been scattered over the floors.

One of the small houses had thousands of small bones from salmon fins in its floor sediments; these elements were rare in the larger houses. Obviously, when Keatley Creek was occupied, some people kept and used the fins for food. Others used them much less. Perhaps the richer houses fed the fins to their dogs, whereas smaller houses without dogs saved the fins for their own soups or snacks. Thus, the butchering, storage, processing, consumption, and discard of salmon is quite varied and complex even within a single village. Food scarcity, local butchering and discard traditions, the specific species of salmon, the extraction of oil, cooking, and the presence of dogs, all seem to play important roles in the understanding of fish bones.

Formation processes associated with deer bones are somewhat more straight forward. Most deer were killed high up in the alpine meadows of the Clear Range Mountains that rise immediately behind the Keatley Creek village. These animals would have been completely butchered in the mountains, their meat cut into thin slices and dried over smokey fires for transport back to the winter village. Only the dried meat, dried skins, and perhaps a few selected pieces of bone or antler for tools would have been brought back to Keatley Creek due to the long, difficult transport and the need to carry other materials such as flaking stone, dried roots, infants, extra clothing, and camping materials.

The vast majority of the deer bones recovered from Keatley Creek were smashed into small pieces. James Teit reported that this was done to extract the marrow and to boil the grease out of the bones. It is highly unlikely that bulky and heavy bones were brought back from the alpine meadows to extract small amounts of grease from them. Thus, the fragmented bones at Keatley Creek probably represent fewer than one or two deer killed during any given winter by the hunters of a particular house as they roamed within a few kilometers of the Keatley Creek village.

Major deposits of dog bones occurred in two large storage pits in the largest house we excavated. Because of the unusual nature of these deposits, I will discuss them later.

BASIC DISTRIBUTIONS

While we have excellent evidence that domestic groups occupied almost the entire perimeter of the largest excavated house (HP 7), the distribution of salmon and deer remains is puzzling. The vast majority of the salmon bones recovered from the floor were found on the right side of the house (Figure 7.2). Does this mean that everyone on the left side of the house went over to the right side of the house to eat their meals, or at least their salmon? This seems impractical and improbable, especially if the fish was stored in pits on the left side of the house and if the largest, most frequent fires were on the left side of the house. Nor does it seem likely that more affluent families with large stores of food and large hearths would cross the house floor to sit and eat with commoners lacking such basic comforts. But what other possibilities could account for this strange distribution? There are several likely suggestions.

First, it is possible that families on the right side of the house ate different types or portions of salmon from their housemates on the left side of the house. Well-to-do families might consume almost exclusively the dried fillets of salmon, just as the most expensive and desirable cuts of meat today are boneless. The backbones of fish might have been relegated to the poorer families in the house since there was less meat on them and it was more difficult to remove from the spiny bones. Alternatively, perhaps poorer families consumed mainly the less desirable pink salmon with bones left in the dried pieces, while richer families ate the boneless sockeye and chinook fillets.

Second, it is possible that much of the daily food preparation was conducted by the poorer or slave residents of the great house. Food preparation was one of the duties of slaves and servants both in the Interior and on the Coast (Teit, 1912a, p. 242; Jewitt, 1974, p. 65; Oberg, 1973, p. 87; Garfield, 1966, p. 29).

Third, it is possible that only the families with large hearths regularly cooked their salmon backbones, thereby reducing the ability of the bones to survive archaeologically in these domestic areas. Families that did not, or could not, make fires on a regular basis might be forced to pick the meat off the backbones without cooking them, and simply discarded the bones afterward.

Fourth, it is possible that poor families in the house were not as conscientious in cleaning up their food wastes as the richer families. Such differences were vividly documented by explorers on the Coast. For instance, Mozino (cited in Samuels, 1991, p. 202) noted the following observation in 1792:

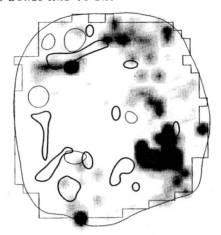

Fish Bone on the Floor of HP 7
Frequencies Range from 0 to 59

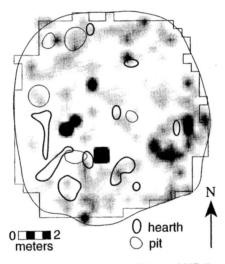

Non–Fish Bone on the Floor of HP 7
Frequencies Range from 0 to 159

FIGURE 7.2. *The distribution of fish bones (top) and non-fish bones across the floor of Housepit 7. All of the identifiable fish bones are salmon and the overwhelming majority of non-fish bones are probably deer. As discussed in the text, these distributions are some of the more curious that were encountered. From Lepofsky et al. (1995).*

Inside . . . of their house they make large fires, clean their fish, and remove shellfish and snails from their shells, leaving a large part of the remains thrown upon the floor where it rots. This causes an unbearable repugnance to anyone who has not grown up in the midst of such stench. The filth is incomparably greater in the houses of the *meschimes* (commoners), both because they are all generally found to be sordid and also because the women do not show the least vestige of what we call cleanliness.

At this point, it is difficult to determine which of the above possible explanations is likely to be correct. However, I would put money on the first one. In this explanation the wealthier families ate mainly boneless sockeye and spring salmon fillets, while the common families ate lower-grade pink salmon with the backbones dried in the fish, or picked off meat from dried sockeye and spring salmon backbones. Intuitively, this seems consistent with the other previously made observations and with present-day rich versus poor eating patterns. Modern Indians of the region, who are no longer faced with starvation, do not even bother to keep the backbones. They are simply thrown away as undesirable food.

The clusters of deer bone fragments in Housepit 7 exhibit another pattern that is perhaps more puzzling (Figure 7.2). We can be relatively certain from the synthetic culture analogy of the area that meat and fat were particularly valued food items, much more highly valued than the abundant salmon. Thus, it might be expected that remains of deer bones would have been concentrated in the left half of the house. However, the actual pattern of deer bones neither corresponds to this expectation, nor to the pattern of fish remains. Instead, there are about five clusters of broken deer bones in various places within the house associated with some hearths, anvils, and concentrations of fire-cracked rocks. Are these clusters the product of differential housecleaning habits of the various families? To answer this, we examined the distribution of small bone fragments on the floor from the bulk soil samples used to collect botanical remains. The small bone fragments almost identically matched the distribution of larger bone fragments (Figure 7.3). Therefore, we were fairly certain that we were monitoring real bone reduction areas, rather than patterns created by cleanup activities. The same, incidentally, is true of the fish bone distributions.

Why should these bone clusters occur around some hearths but not others, and why should these clusters occur on both the right and the left sides of the large house? It may have been due to two or three different domestic groups gathering together around a single hearth to prepare the meat from a newly killed deer. A fresh deer kill must have been an important occasion for celebrating, since it would have occurred rarely during the winter. In Coastal houses, such as those recovered at Ozette in Washington State, a similar pattern of three to four concentrations of faunal remains occurs (Figure 7.4), even though there is evidence for twice that number of domestic groups residing within the structure (Samuels, 1991). Perhaps there was frequently more cooperation in cooking large game between closely affiliated families than we imagine.

Although, ethnographically, the best hunters were considered rich—and frequently obtained special training because they were from rich families—more common families were not barred from hunting and might accompany the trained hunters. Any game killed was reportedly divided among all the participating hunters. This, too, may account for the limited number of bone clusters on both sides of the house. Perhaps only men from these domestic groups participated in the winter hunts, and therefore returned back with bones to process. Marrow was almost certainly highly valued, and it seems possible that the highest ranking hunters would have claimed the main marrow bones for themselves. However, once these bones had been broken open and the marrow extracted, the remaining bone material might

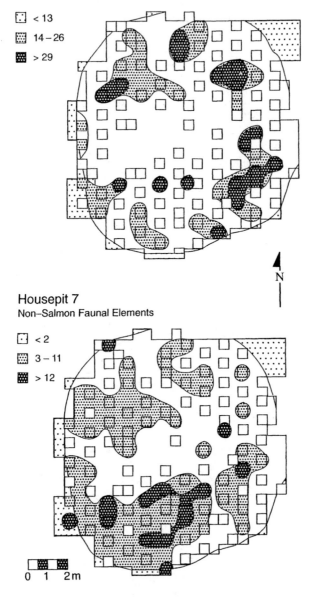

Housepit 7 EeR1–7
Salmon (NISP) /1 Liter Sample

- ⬚ < 13
- ⬚ 14 – 26
- ⬛ > 29

N

Housepit 7
Non–Salmon Faunal Elements

- ⬚ < 2
- ⬚ 3 – 11
- ⬛ > 12

0 1 2 m

FIGURE 7.3. *In order to test the accuracy of the fish and non-fish bone distributions obtained through standard screening techniques using 6 mm mesh screens, we examined the small fractions of bones that were contained in the heavy residue of the flotation samples using a 1 mm mesh screen. There is, in fact, a very high degree of correspondence between the two distributions indicating not only that the results of the larger mesh screen provided reliable results, but also that housecleaning or scuffage that generally affects larger wastes had not significantly altered the distribution of bones on the floor.*

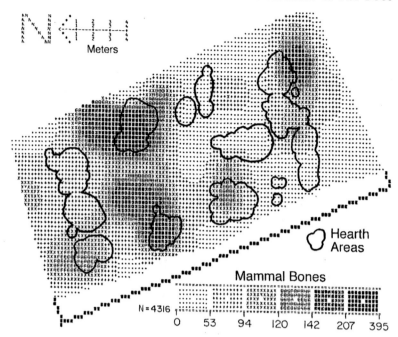

FIGURE 7.4. *While there are clearly 6 to 8 domestic groups in Housepit 7 based on the number of hearths associated with clusters of fire-cracked rock, debitage, and artifacts, there are only about half that number of bone concentrations on the floor. This represents one of the puzzling aspects of the bone distributions on the floors. However, this same pattern has also been documented by David Huelsbeck (1994) in the floors of some Coastal houses such as this high-status house floor at Ozette. These patterns may indicate that although each domestic group had and used its own "kitchen" on some occasions, for most daily meals, several domestic groups may have joined together for meal preparation, perhaps in order to conserve fuel or for other reasons.*

have been given to lower ranking families to extract grease through the more laborious technique of smashing and boiling. In a similar fashion, it appears that plantation owners in the southern United States systematically gave their slaves leftover bones from meals, presumably for use in soups (Crader, 1990).

At this point, these explanations are somewhat speculative. In order to understand exactly what the clustering of bone fragments means within the housepits at Keatley Creek, it will be necessary to excavate other large houses and to develop ways to test the various possible explanations of bone distributions. The same is true for the understanding of the clustering of salmon remains.

THE MYSTERY OF THE DOGS

There is another, more intriguing, enigma that has not been solved. It involves the remains of nine dogs buried at the bottom of two large storage pits in the largest housepit we excavated (HP 7). Some of the dogs were represented only by skulls or jaws; some of the dogs had been dismembered; and one of the dogs was put in the pit intact (Figure 7.5). Why had these dogs been buried in such a fashion?

Ethnographic information recorded by Simon Fraser and James Teit offers several suggestions. When Simon Fraser passed through the Lillooet region in 1808, his men were repeatedly given dogs to eat by the chiefs they came in contact with. Thus, dogs may have been used as a special feasting food, just as on the Great Plains and among various other groups in North America (Kerber, 1995) and elsewhere. James Teit (1909) also recorded accounts of a Dog Dance society ritual in which members worked themselves into a rabid frenzy and then attacked a living dog, tearing it to pieces, much as Dionysian maenads were reported to have done to animals in classical Greece. Similar societies existed on the Northwest Coast, while other Pacific Coastal groups such as the Koryak in Northeast Asia sacrificed dogs particularily during the winter, putting their bodies on poles outside their pithouses.

Were the dogs at Keatley Creek buried as part of a feast or ritual? There were other indications that dogs might have a special ritual status. In the middle of the floor of Housepit 7, a dog skull had been left prior to the burning of the structure. In the middle of a medium-sized housepit, most of the body of an immature dog had been left in the center of the floor before that structure had been burned. In another smaller housepit, the charred bones of a dog occurred in the center of the floor. Elsewhere, at Bridge River near Lillooet, in a substantial housepit, a large storage pit was discovered to contain the remains of about four dogs (Langemann, 1987, p. 156–158). At Monte Creek, along the Thompson River, in the oldest housepit discovered in British Columbia (ca. 4500 B.P.), the remains of a complete dog were left in the center of the floor (Wilson, 1992, p. 132–133). At Wildcat Canyon, Oregon, near The Dalles, six complete dogs had been carefully arranged and buried in a large pit, apparently as part of a sacrifice (Dumond & Minor, 1983, pp. 115–116). Ethnographically, dog sacrifices were also common on the British Columbia Plateau, but usually as part of their owners' funerals (Teit, 1906, pp. 269–270; 1909, p. 593). It is interesting that when sacrificed ethnographically, dogs were often suspended from poles.

David Crellin undertook a special and thorough analysis of all dog remains from Keatley Creek. There was no doubt that the dogs involved were domesticated, rather than wild. The dog at Monte Creek was also domesticated, even though it was over 3,000 years older than the dogs at Keatley Creek. Moreover, these dogs appear to have been domesticated from coyotes rather than wolves, the origin of almost all other domesticated dogs.

One of the first things Crellin observed were a number of deformities in the spines of two dogs. These corresponded to the kinds of deformities common in pack animals, and, in fact, there are ethnographic accounts and photographs of dogs being used to carry up to 80 pounds on their backs. There can be no doubt that some of the dogs at Keatley Creek were being used for hauling heavy loads. They were later replaced by horses, which became known as "dog-deer." Ethnographically, other dogs were valued for hunting, while still others were probably of little practical use and were treated as vagrants. Crellin discovered another important feature: A very large percentage of the dog bones had been chewed and gnawed by other carnivores, presumably by other dogs living at Keatley Creek. The evidence was indisputable,

FIGURE 7.5. *Two of the large storage pits in Housepit 7 contained the remains of numerous dogs at the bottom including this entirely intact skeleton of a dog that had been used for packing heavy loads. Some dogs were represented only by their skulls (one is visible at the upper right), others were disarticulated into leg and back segments. Clearly, these are very unusual deposits most probably representing special rituals.*

but how could this have happened? Crellin thought it would have been improbable for people to have left sacrificed dog remains in their houses for the time necessary to have resulted in the extensive degree of gnawing that he observed. He therefore began to explore the possibility that the dogs may have died naturally after having entered the houses when people left them in the spring.

Before interpreting archaeological remains as evidence for rituals or any unusual behavior, it is first necessary to rule out possible natural occurrences. As Crellin subsequently noted, there are several indications that the dogs in these pits did not simply move in after residents left, then die, and undergo cannibalization by the remaining dogs.

First, there are no identifiable dog bones in the rest of the floor deposits, except for the skull in the center. If dogs had gnawed and broken their comrades' bones while on the floor, a few fragments should certainly have escaped the cleanup crew.

Second, while a high percentage of the dogs' bones showed clear evidence of gnawing, virtually none of the hundreds of deer or other bones on the house floors showed evidence of gnawing. If dogs had penetrated the houses to scavenge scraps of food as well as to cannibalize their comrades, they certainly should have gnawed the deer bones left behind. The lack of gnawed bones on the floor is consistent with Interior tales and myths which describe the dogs as being kept outside the pithouses rather than inside (Teit, 1912a, p. 250, 256, 307; 1912b, p. 325; 1917, p. 46).

Third, if the dogs had been left behind because they were unwanted and worthless, and if people discovered dog remains on the housepit floors when they returned several months later, it seems logical to expect them to throw out the gnawed dog remains together with all the other materials they removed when cleaning up the house before reoccupying it in the fall. As we saw in chapter 3, housecleaning remains were generally thrown on the rim. Yet, these dogs were dealt with in a very different fashion; they were buried in storage pits. Moreover, the dirt matrix which contained the dog bones contained little else—no other kinds of garbage one might expect from the floor, just a large number of dog bones.

Fourth, the soil matrix in which the dog remains were found was not like the black soil so typical of floor deposits. Instead, it was brownish and had little else in it. Where had this soil come from, if not the floor?

None of these observations is consistent with a naturally occurring, scavenged death assemblage originating inside the housepit. Moreover, at least one of the skulls shows clear evidence of a killing blow to the head, and one or two of the skulls were more weathered than the others, indicating exposure over time outside of the house. The bulk of these observations indicate the dog remains had been outside for at least a period of some months. This is shown by the degree of scavenging and gnawing; the weathering; and the soil matrix which is typical of soils around the housepits, but not of housepit sediments themselves. There is also evidence of possible sacrifice or killing of dogs, indicated by the blows to the dogs' heads, the burial of an entire dog, and a number of articulated limbs. It is therefore possible that some of the dog remains in the pits represent dogs that were sacrificed and then displayed on poles outside the pithouse, much as the Koryak did, or as the historic Interior Salish did over graves. Outside the houses, they would have been subject to disarticulation from decay and predation by dogs that roamed the village. Perhaps at a Dog Dance ceremony, one or more additional dogs were sacrificed. Periodic collection and burial of all sacrificed dog remains may have been a part of the ritual. Many tribal groups in China and Southeast Asia display the jaws, skulls, or horns of the most valuable domestic animals (buffalo or pigs). They place these bones on their houses in ways resembling what may have happened at Keatley Creek (Kim, 1994, p. 121; Leach, 1954, p. 118; Junker et al., 1994, p. 321; Hayden, 1996, field notes). These displayed pig and buffalo bones were also gathered and disposed of periodically, especially when houses were rebuilt.

In the British Columbia Interior, ethnographers point out that people disposed of animal bones in water so dogs would not chew them and offend the animal spirits. Archaeologists are fond of pointing out that there are still many animal bones at sites like Keatley Creek. But in any event, the frozen ground and water at this site during the winter may have precluded disposing of spiritually important dog bones in any other way than gathering them together to bury in a pit inside the houses.

We still do not know exactly what the many dogs in Housepit 7 represent in terms of actual behavior. The issue is more complex than we had originally anticipated, but we have uncovered some of the most important clues necessary to deciphering this riddle. If a ritual ceremony was involved, as I think it probably was, then it may have been performed in certain houses either because of their clan totemic history, or because of membership in a special canid crest group, or because of the different abilities to display wealth and success using dogs and large feasts. I feel certain that whatever practical roles some of the dogs filled, the keeping, feeding, breeding, and even the killing of dogs must have been a form of prestige display that only the wealthy could have afforded on a sustained basis. In their roles as beasts of burden, as hunters, and as live sacrifices, dogs were probably the original slaves of these complex hunters and gatherers. They were also the only animal to have been domesticated throughout most of North America. It seems likely that their initial domestication began among complex hunter–gatherers throughout the world because these people had the surplus food to sustain feeding and breeding these animals (costs which were substantial), and because only complex hunter–gatherers had the motivation to use such animals for prestige display purposes. Generalized hunter–gatherers sometimes captured pups of wild dogs to keep as pets or even aides in hunting, but there were few costs involved since the wild dogs foraged for themselves and did not have to be kept on a sustained basis (see Hayden, 1975). In contrast, as Kerber (1995) has also observed, domesticating dogs requires the keeping and breeding of dogs in an unbroken chain of generations. Domesticated dogs do not forage for themselves. They must therefore be fed by people. Wild dogs may have been used as pets for many thousands of years before they were domesticated, but it was only the economic and social conditions of complex hunter–gatherers that led to their feeding, breeding, and domestication.

PRESTIGE CREATURES

As can be seen from the example of dogs, members of the animal kingdom were not used just for food. They also played important roles in displaying wealth, prestige, and power. Furs, feathers, and fine leathers were all valuable animal prestige items that would not preserve very well. However, we can infer their presence from the recovery of claw bones left attached to furs (Teit, 1906, p. 257), wing bones that were part of feather displays, and from the specialized stone tools that were used to make buckskin. Thus, it is clear that some residents in Housepit 7 had at least bear, lynx, beaver, and red fox skins. Wing bones from hawks were also recovered. And a cache of spall scrapers used in producing buckskin was found against the wall on the northwest (left) side of the house.

However, there are also remains of animals used more directly for display. From a storage pit in one house, we recovered a set of 72 bone buttons that apparently had been sewn onto a skin. Pieces of bone had also been thinned or smoothed and then decorated with carved or incised lines, undoubtedly for wearing as jewelry (Figure 7.6). Two antlers had been cut and tapered, possibly for use in a headdress. There was also a surprising array of marine animals represented, including numerous dentalium shells, a piece of a bracelet made from a purple-hinged rock scallop, and a shaped piece of mussel shell. At the nearby and contemporaneous Bell site, a club made of whalebone, a pectin shell rattle, a number of bone carvings, and over 200 dentalium shells were recovered. These were associated with the single burial encountered at the site, that of a child. All of these must have been prestige items and required substantial amounts of surplus wealth to obtain. They either required great effort to make or had to be brought many hundreds of kilometers over

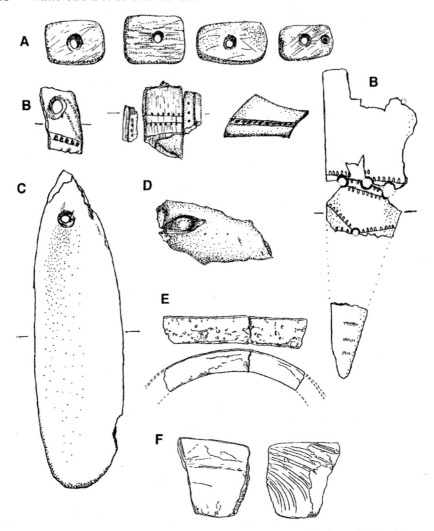

FIGURE 7.6. *Some of the prestige bone artifacts that were recovered from Keatley Creek include 72 bone buttons that were probably all sewn onto a single garment for decoration (A), shaped and incised pendants probably used as jewelry (B), a bullroarer (C), an eye that was part of a larger sculpture (D), part of a bracelet made of purple-hinged rock scallop from the Coast (E), and part of a mussel shell adze from the Coast (F). The antler digging-stick handle and bark peeler in Figure 2.2 were probably prestige items also.*

the mountains from the coast. These objects were probably displayed prominently before invited guests during major winter feasts and ritual performances. In the energetic dancing and drumming, it is not surprising that a few items might have broken off costumes and been lost in the floor dust. The presence of these objects shows that the large Classic Lillooet communities were quite complex for hunter–gatherers and that considerable inequalities in wealth and power must have existed within these societies.

BONE TOOLS

Bones were also used for more practical purposes. The most common type of bone tool that we found was the bone awl. Ethnographically, these were used for puncturing skin or bark to sew clothing or containers, and for piercing ears and noses of high-ranking children. The sandstone abraders associated with each domestic area in Housepit 7 were undoubtedly used to sharpen these awls. A number of deer shoulder blades were also cut and sharpened along one edge, apparently to use as a knife or scraper of soft materials, but we do not as yet know how or on what material they were used.

The bases of large antlers were used as billets for making the large bifacial knives used throughout much of prehistoric North America. While antler billets are surprisingly rare archaeologically, we recovered two examples of these tools. Antler was also used to make digging-stick handles (see Figure 2.2). However, because of the rarity of antler and its hardness, most digging-stick handles were probably made of hard wood, just as they were up until recent times. This indicates that antler handles may have been used by high-ranking women as a display of affluence. Similarly, we recovered a bark peeler made out of antler, whereas all recorded ethnographic examples were made of hard wood. This may have also been a prestige item.

What is interesting are the tools we did not recover. Given the overwhelming importance of salmon fishing for the Lillooet communities, we expected to find abundant remains of fishing tools. However, out of the thousands of artifacts recovered in our excavations at Keatley Creek, there were only three fishing objects found. These were two barbed bone points and a possible net needle. It seems clear that either all the fishing tools were made of more perishable materials such as wood, or that all the fishing gear was left at fishing locations by the river. This does not accord well with Lewis Binford's models of collectors using "curated" tools. According to Binford (1973, p. 242, 249–250), curated tools used at resource procurement locations should have been returned to the main base camps for storage and repair, where they became part of the archaeological record. We have only the scantiest evidence this was done at all. The absence of fishing implements at Keatley Creek is surprising, but incontrovertible.

DIFFERENCES BETWEEN HOUSEPITS

There are a number of important differences between housepits in terms of bone remains. The most important difference for understanding the social and economic organization at Keatley Creek involved the types of salmon bones recovered. In a radiographic study of the salmon backbones found in the floor deposits and storage pits, Kevin Berry was able to determine that the small housepits used exclusively pink salmon. Pink salmon are the smallest, weakest, and the easiest to procure in the region. They swim close to the riverbanks and have the least amount of fat. Ethnographically, pink salmon were considered poor quality food. In contrast to the small houses, the larger houses had a mix of salmon types. They used a great deal of pink salmon, but they also had substantial amounts of the more desired and highly valued sockeye and spring salmon (Figure 7.7).

This finding meant several important things. It meant that not everyone had equal access to the best fishing rocks jutting far out into the Fraser River where the deep-swimming sockeye and spring salmon could be obtained with the help of platforms or scaffolds. Some form of ownership of resource locations must have existed. Such a conclusion demonstrated that there was an important continuity between prehistoric practices and the ethnographic observations of owned fishing locations (see Romanoff, 1992a; Kennedy & Bouchard, 1992). Kevin Berry's analysis also demonstrated that there was a major difference in the economic foundations of the large versus the smaller housepits, with the larger housepits controlling the most important surplus-producing resource locations. This was a giant step in our understanding of the social and economic organization at Keatley Creek and, in fact, corroborated Lewis Henry Morgan's (1881) early opinion that members of residential corporate groups were motivated by economic reasons to act as a unit.

There were other differences in the bone remains between housepits. Karla Kusmer's analysis indicated the smaller houses had fewer fish and mammal bones, in lower densities on the floors, and there were fewer different types of animals being used in small houses than in the larger houses (Table 7.1). These results parallel the lower diversity of plants associated with small houses. These results indicate that occupants of smaller houses had less meat than occupants of the great houses, and that they used few if any animals for prestige or technological purposes. Residents of poorer, small houses probably concentrated on the most practical types of game that were readily available. The bones of fish may have been almost entirely consumed by people of these houses, either in soups or pounded up for other dishes.

In small housepits, such as Housepit 12 where probably four nuclear families lived, there is only one small, superficial hearth area, one concentration of fire-cracked rock, and one concentration of bone material near the hearth. In contrast to the large housepits where each domestic group seems to have had its own cooking, sleeping, and work areas, the residents of smaller houses seem to have done most activities in a single communal area. There is no sign of separate family areas, no indication of hierarchy in the smaller housepits, and there is no indication of surplus being stored or any other sign of wealth. The more limited resources that smaller housepits had to work with are certainly consistent with a more communal and egalitarian ethic as discussed in chapter 1.

One small housepit (HP 9) was unique among the rest. This was a small structure located across the creek from the core of the site, almost isolated on the southern periphery. This house had an unusual amount of storage capacity for its size. It had the only stone-lined hearth discovered anywhere in the site, it had greater amounts of antler than in any other house (including the only antler digging-stick handle and bark peeler we recovered at the site), it had the greatest amount of dentalium and shell recovered from any housepit, it had the only loon and bald eagle bones recovered anywhere in the site, and it had pipe fragments and parts of a nephrite adze. Loon bones were a special find, as they were used by shamans in some Interior Salish groups (Teit, 1900, p. 381; 1909, p. 607). All this indicates unusual wealth and prestige for the occupants. Was this the residence of a successful and

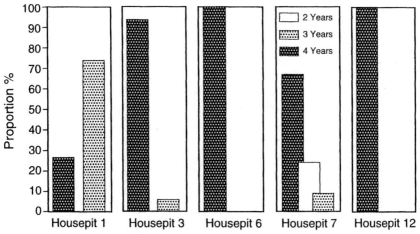

FIGURE 7.7. *Top: The proportion of different species of salmon in each housepit reveals a great deal about its economic status. In his analysis, Kevin Berry (1991) found that small housepits such as HP 6 and HP 12 have exclusively pink salmon, which spawns at two years of age. Pink salmon are the smallest, driest, and least desirable species of salmon. They can be caught in many locations along the river banks. Large housepits such as HP 1 and HP 7 have significant proportions of salmon that spawned at three and four years of age. These correspond most closely to the sockeye and chinook salmon, which are the largest, fattest, and most valuable type of salmon, which are accessible only from special jetties and platforms. Ethnographically, these special fishing spots were owned and the prehistoric distribution of salmon species among housepits seems to indicate that the same was true in the past.*

Bottom: The age at which salmon spawn and die can be determined by counting the annual growth rings in the vertebrae. In the x-rayed examples shown here, four growth rings are clearly visible.

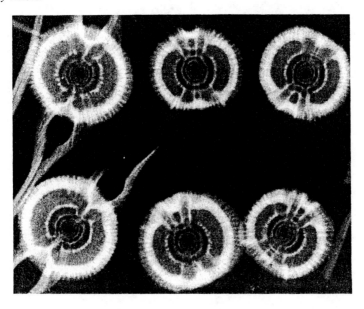

wealthy hunter or perhaps of a shaman affiliated with one of the great houses? Why did the occupants live so far from most people at the site? Perhaps there are other examples of such residences at Keatley Creek and we will be able to answer these questions in the future. For the time being, it is clear that this was the home of a distinctive household that has added another important dimension to our understanding of the social and economic organization of the prehistoric Keatley Creek community. We will discuss more of its role in the community in chapter 8.

SUMMARY

Studying bones tells archaeologists what was eaten by the denizens of prehistory. It also provides important information about how people arrayed themselves to display their success, what the social and economic divisions and inequalities were within the communities, how tools were used in daily activities, and it also reveals some of the less understood facets of rituals and ceremonies. We have also seen how bones can add important information on formation processes and how complex the formation of bone assemblages can be.

In the realm of ritual, there are enough indications to show that some unusual activities involving dogs were taking place. It is extremely difficult, if not impossible, to account for all the dog remains left in the centers of housepits and all the dogs buried in large storage pits as primarily reflecting natural formation processes. However, the precise nature of dog rituals cannot be ascertained at this point. Further examples are necessary to make progress in unraveling the mystery of the dogs. I am convinced that dogs are pivotal in our understanding of domestication since they were the first domesticated animal in most parts of the world. They were domesticated among complex hunter–gatherers beginning about 10,000 years ago; and they were the only domesticated animal throughout most of North America. I suspect the ability to support dogs with surplus food and their role in status display is a key ingredient to understanding this development. Domesticated dogs are primarily associated with complex rather than generalized hunter–gatherers for this reason, and it is also among complex hunter–gatherers that feasting becomes economically and politically important for the first time. Like dogs, these feasts are intimately related to surplus accumulations and status displays, but this is a topic to be broached in the next chapter.

CHAPTER 8

Big Man, Little Man, Beggar Man, Feast

The factual differences between the housepits at Keatley Creek have been clearly set out and explored. While some small houses, such as Housepit 9, may have been occupied by individuals who were wealthy because of their specialized roles or their connections to larger, more powerful households, most small houses were occupied by relatively impoverished domestic groups that had poorer quality and less salmon, meat, and plant foods. The prestige items in most small households were rare or of poor quality. Activities within small houses seem to have been communal undertakings, although probably divided according to sex. In short, there is no evidence of much surplus, wealth, hierarchy, or specialization within most of the small households.

On the other hand, the largest residential corporate structure that was excavated yielded great amounts of storage per person and has repeated indications of accumulated lucre in the form of shells from the coast, remains of animals used for prestige displays and showpiece rituals, worked nephrite and copper, pipes, dogs, and specially sculpted or shaped stone and bone pieces. Moreover, many sorts of evidence indicate that there was a fundamental division within the house between the corporate descendants of the house owners and poorer working families. While families on both sides of the house had hearths accompanied by anvils, abrading stones, fire-cracked rocks, stone tools, stone debitage, and bedding materials, only the domestic groups on one side of the house had large hearths accompanied by large storage pits. This division of the house into an elite half and a poor half corresponds in a remarkable way to James Teit's observation that one-half to two-thirds of the ethnographic communities were elite families (see chapter 2). There also appears to be one hearth area in the large house that was more "administrative" than labor oriented, and this may have been the domestic area of the headman of the corporate group.

From the analysis of salmon remains, it is clear that the large corporate groups had priviledged access, if not ownership, of the most economically important fishing sites. This accords well with the ethnographic accounts of such sites being owned and inherited, usually with rights extending to closely related men. Ethnographically, it is clear that the elites of such corporate groups also tried to restrict access to the most important and valued hunted game, sometimes probably by promoting their own sons as the only qualified people capable of leading hunting parties due to their lengthy (and costly) practical and spiritual training. Elites also restricted access to deer by successfully claiming ownership of deer fences that they constructed and sometimes by simply trying to claim ownership of the best hunting territories (see Romanoff, 1992b; Dawson, 1892, p. 14; Teit, 1909). This may be the significance behind the greater amounts of deer bone remains in the largest house compared to any other excavated house at the site. In this fashion, consumption of deer meat could be used as a demonstration of economic and spiritual superiority.

But there is another indication that the large corporate groups held privileged access to hunting and root-gathering areas in the mountains behind the site, if they did not own these areas outright. This added piece of the prehistoric puzzle comes from the analysis of the many-hued bits of colored stone chipping debris that were found discarded at the housepits. How can stone debitage tell archaeologists that members of specific residential corporate groups owned hunting territories in the mountains? The trail of evidence is not entirely obvious at the outset. In fact, we stumbled upon it by accident while looking at stone debitage from various housepits for other reasons. In the process of looking at these bits of stone waste material, it became evident that there were some major differences between housepits in terms of the cherts and chalcedonies associated with each dwelling (Figure 8.1). A detailed petrographic analysis by Edward Bakewell confirmed the validity of the distinctive types of chert and chalcedony that were initially established by visual criteria alone. Since we knew that all the large housepits were occupied over the same period of time, these differences did not seem to reflect changes through time. What else could they represent?

In order to determine where the various cherts and chalcedonies were coming from, Mike Rousseau conducted a survey of the entire foraging range that the residents of Keatley Creek probably used during their yearly movements. He succeeded in locating the general source areas for a number of types of cherts and chalcedonies used at Keatley Creek. All of these sources were in mountain areas that are ethnographically used by the present-day Fraser River Indians near Keatley Creek for hunting and gathering mountain plant foods such as lily roots and mountain potatoes. Different kinds of cherts were found in different parts of the mountains. The conclusion seemed inescapable that the residents of each great house were going to separate parts of the mountains to hunt and gather plant foods. While there, they must have also gathered suitable cobbles and cores for making stone tools and brought these back to their winter village. There is little overlap between some houses that used these stone types. This implies a relatively exclusive use of mountain areas by the residents of different housepits rather than a free-ranging, communal, and changeable use. Our data indicated something approaching ownership in terms of the corporate groups' control over those mountain areas. It is therefore very interesting to note that Dawson (1892, p. 14) recorded that the Shuswap formerly had owned hereditary family hunting grounds.

Some generalized hunter–gatherers, such as those reported by Richard Gould in central Australia (Gould & Saggers, 1985), transported exotic raw materials from distant locations. The materials were from their ancestral lands and helped maintain links between distant groups for alliance purposes. However, at Keatley Creek, the stone sources were *within* the area used by the community and there would have been no other groups occupying these lands. Residents of Keatley Creek may well have had ideological attachments to their stone sources, but it is clear they also had

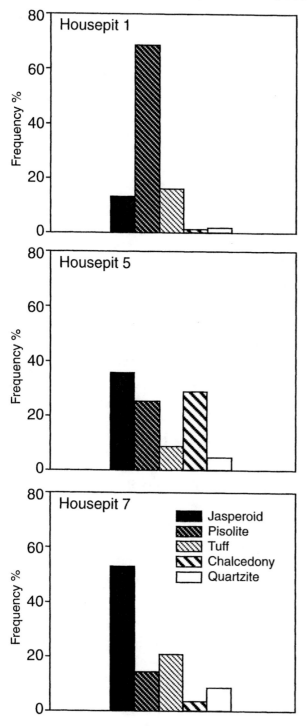

FIGURE 8.1. *These graphs represent the varying proportions of different types of cherts recovered from Housepits 1, 5, and 7. There are only a few distinctive types of chert and chalcedony that occur in any substantial frequency in the large housepits that were tested or excavated. However, the differences in the use of these sources between houses is striking. Residents of Housepit 1 primarily relied on a distinctive type of speckled chert (pisolite) throughout its entire history from the Shuswap period deposits at the bottom of the rim until the last occupation floor. In contrast, residents of Housepit 7 primarily relied on a yellowish jasper chert from the Hat Creek Valley throughout its entire history while the inhabitants of Housepit 5 used far more chalcedony than in either of the other large houses. These results indicate that each of these houses retained its own corporate identity and control of different mountain resource areas for over 1,000 years, which is perhaps the longest documented persistence of any corporate group on record. From Hayden et al. (1996).*

economic and practical reasons for using those lands. Those uses and ideologies caused partitioning of the landscape by the major corporate groups of Keatley Creek.

However, there were more surprises in store for us in these observations. When we began to look at the chert types in the roof deposits and in the rim middens associated with each large house, it became clear that for the large housepits these patterns persisted throughout their entire history of refuse accumulation (see Hayden et al., 1996). This had startling ramifications. It not only reinforced the notion that ownership of key mountain areas had been present at Keatley Creek, but also that the social and economic groups that possessed these rights had persisted from the beginnings of the rim midden accumulations in Shuswap times (3500–2400 B.P.) until the time the houses were abandoned around 1000 B.P. *Minimally*, that represents a period of over 1,400 years.

The indication that specific prehistoric corporate groups among hunter–gatherers could have lasted this long seemed unbelievable, and was certainly unheard of in the ambient opinion of the time. We literally had found the longest lasting corporate group ever recorded in the world under our feet. But there was still more.

Our analysis also indicated that ownership of the large house sites must have been maintained throughout this same period. It is inconceivable that such long-term house site ownership did not entail reoccupation of the house from year to year by the same corporate group for over a thousand years. This is entirely consistent with the stratified nature of the rim deposits, in which no major temporal breaks can be discerned. It is also consistent with the unchanging patterns of deep postholes and large storage pits observed in the floor of Housepit 7 (see chapter 4). If the large houses had been abandoned for any significant length of time and then reoccupied, it would have been unlikely for the new occupants to choose the exact same places to dig their deep postholes and storage pits. However, almost all main postholes and storage pits conform to the same basic pattern, as though a continuous tradition was being followed.

The above conclusions were so revolutionary that I wanted to be sure there was not a fatal flaw in the analysis. We therefore excavated additional parts of the rims of the large housepits involved in the study to obtain a larger sample. We also analyzed the cherts on three separate occasions using different individuals and differing levels of precision in the classification of the cherts. All the analyses were independent and "blind" in relation to each other. The results came out essentially the same in all cases. The conclusions therefore seem extremely robust and cannot be dismissed as spurious.

MECHANISMS OF CHANGE AND HIERARCHIES

In terms of firm, well-founded conclusions, we have now established that there were large residential corporate groups that controlled the best fishing sites and the best mountain resource areas, that amassed food surplus and wealth, and that created hierarchical relationships both within their houses and between other houses. But how did all this come about from a basis of egalitarian hunter–gatherers who must have existed prior to the establishment of pithouses? What was the mechanism and the means by which these developments came into being? Here we depart from the "tight" interpretations of the actual archaeological observations presented in preceding pages, and we begin to delve into the realm of grander theories that are much more difficult to prove or disprove because they deal in such extensive generalities. However, such ideas are necessary to explore if we are ever to find out whether there are underlying principles that govern human behavior and cultural evolution.

There are many ideas about how social, economic, and political hierarchies emerge from more egalitarian types of societies. They include simple population growth and pressures; simple, increasingly complex mechanics of community organization with increasing community sizes; the need to make rapid decisions for survival and for waging effective warfare; internal transmutations of the social values or the ideological bases within a culture; the ability of some individuals to extort surpluses from others when labor-intensive improvements tie people to specific places; the usefulness of elites in times of famine or other crises; and the ability of ambitious individuals with more surpluses to lure other community members into lopsided contractual obligations. These and various other ideas can be put into three basic categories:

1. Explanations that view people as being forced into accepting hierarchies (due to population pressures, extortion, warfare, or other factors);

2. explanations that view people as being lured into hierarchies (by promises of sharing in wealth or obtaining other desirable advantages);

3. explanations that seem to be related to random, "black box" events, such as changes in cultural values, social relationships, or genetic mutations leading to domestication.

Debates surrounding these issues are more appropriate for specialized and advanced treatises. Rather than enter into the labyrinthine arguments involved in their discussion, I will simply present the scenario that I feel makes the most sense in general, and at Keatley Creek in particular. Those interested in following the detailed arguments may consult previous publications (Hayden, 1995).

As argued in the opening chapter of this book, hierarchies do not seem to flourish under conditions of duress, that is, conditions that frequently result in malnutrition, sickness, and death due to scarcity of food. Certainly on the Northwest Coast and in the Northwest Interior, there is an extremely strong relationship between abundant resources that are invulnerable to overexploitation, and the development of social and political complexity (Donald & Mitchell, 1975; Hayden, 1992). The same is true in New Guinea (Feil, 1987), Southeast Asia (Leach, 1954), and undoubtedly many other places. The ability to produce, and probably store, surplus items seems to be an essential condition for most developments of complexity. Although monopolistic trade may be a secondary condition that can promote complexity in otherwise poor environments, as in the case of the Owens Valley Paiute (Bettinger, 1978, 1983) and some Carrier groups (Goldman, 1940) and the high mountain passes of Burma (Leach, 1954).

Mesolithic types of technology were probably required to procure and store resources in such abundance, which is why complex hunter–gatherers do not occur prior to the Mesolithic (15000–5000 B.P.), Archaic (10000–3000 B.P.), or late Upper Paleolithic periods (25000–10000 B.P.). The empirical relation between abundant resources and social complexity seems relatively well established. It can be documented ethnographically from Coastal Peru to California, Alaska, Siberia, Florida, and Australia. It can be documented prehistorically in these same areas, as well as many North American riverine Archaic groups, European Mesolithic groups, and among the Near Eastern Natufians.

I have argued that general members of egalitarian communities will recognize claims of ownership over prime resources only when they have enough food for themselves, or when they do not feel threatened by other people having exclusive rights to the exploitation of important resources (Hayden, 1996). But how can surplus be converted into political power and economic benefits, especially if everyone has enough food for themselves in egalitarian types of societies? Because of the high degree of patterning associated with these developments (notably their lack of occurrence during the preceding 2 million years, and their strong association with abundant resources and specific types of technology), I do not think the notion of hierarchies emerging due to random events is tenable. If people were not being pushed into hierarchical relationships by resource shortages, then they must have been lured.

Ambitious, self-centered people could have used excess foods for their own personal gain. They undoubtedly began to develop schemes to use other people's surplus to increase their own wealth, power, and well-being—in short, to increase their own chances of survival and fitness. Such prospects may have motivated aggrandizers to invest heavily in schemes to separate productive people from the fruits of their labor. What were the lures that ambitious people could have used? I suggest that there are many strategies that prospective "aggrandizers" (ambitious, aggressive, accumulative, "triple-A" personality types) used in order to get other people to produce surplus food and then surrender control of some of that surplus to the aggrandizers (Table 8.1). Here, I will focus only on feasts, marriage payments, and child growth payments. For many years, Marvin Harris (1985) has emphasized the key role that "Big Men," feasting, and warfare have played in these developments. My approach is very similar to his and owes much to his insights. The underlying principle that made all of these strategies work was the contractual agreement, or debt, whether this was a pledge to the community at large to provide food or other items for a common purpose, or whether it was a pledge between individuals, families, or corporate groups. Without binding contractual agreements, few people might honor agreements to produce or surrender surplus food or wealth items. Debts between individuals, families, or corporate groups typically took the form of feasts and gifts.

The respect for the opinions and wishes of gift givers is notoriously short-lived, especially when there is no immediate prospect for future gifts. Most readers can probably remember incidents in their own lives where open generosity, lacking other constraints, has resulted only in subsequent ingratitude if not abuse of the giver. This behavior may not be universal in our own society, but it is certainly common. Such behavior was also common in more traditional societies where aggrandizers wanted to obtain wealth gifts but did not want to obey any higher authority

TABLE 8.1
THE MOST COMMON STRATEGIES USED BY
TRANSEGALITARIAN AGGRANDIZERS TO INCREASE CONTROL

Aggrandizer Strategies	Egalitarian	Despots	Reciprocators	Entrepreneurs	Chiefdoms
Territorial conquest					......X|XXXXXXXXX
Provoked war (extortion/death compensation)		....x|XXXXXXXXX	XXXXXXXXXX	xxxxxxxxxx.|.............	
Bridewealth			.....................|xxxxxxxxxxxx	xXXXXXX	Elite / Non-elite
Obligatory initiations	xxxxxxxXX|XXXXXXXXXX	Xxxxx............	....		Elite
Childgrowth		..|.....xxxxxxxxX	XXXXXXXX|		Non-elite
Investment		..|...................xx	xxXXXXXXXX|Xxx....		
Feasts					
Solidarity	XXXXXXX|XXXxxxxxxxx	....	....		
Reciprocal exchange	....x|xxxxxxxXXX	XXXXXXXXXX|Xxxxxxxxxx		
Competitive				....XXXXxxxxxx..	(Elite only)
Cults: Ancestors and others		..|...................|.xxxxxxxxxxxx	xxxxxxxxxxxxx|XXXXX	

(e.g., Helms, 1994, p. 56). Thus, if surpluses or wealth were to be used to increase aggrandizers' self-benefit, contractual agreements involving some types of gifts were essential.

It should be mentioned that there is a profound difference in the way social anthropologists versus cultural ecologists view aggrandizers. Social anthropologists are usually concerned mainly with kinship systems and cognitive structures. The implicit or explicit position of these anthropologists is that people in traditional societies who give away great amounts of wealth do it simply to achieve greater prestige or status. For social anthropologists, the motivating factor for the desire to give away wealth appears to be the psychological gratification that comes from favorable things people might say about these benefactors. In this view, there are no necessary practical benefits of gift giving; any practical benefits are at best incidental side effects. For instance, any increased political influence derived from giving gifts might simply stem from the "respect" that other community members have for people who give away wealth.

In contrast, cultural ecologists argue that if people *systematically* (versus the idiosyncratic behavior of individuals) give away substantial amounts of wealth, this can make sense only in terms of achieving some practical benefit for the givers. Practical benefits can include the obligatory return of the gifts (often together with interest payments), the establishment of alliances for wealth exchanges or military purposes, the attraction of productive supporters or mates through lavish promotional displays of success (advertising), the more effective operation of an economic organization due to cooperation between members, and paying off some individuals for their acquiescence to events and claims so that they do not become disgruntled and create problems for aggrandizers. All of these situations have implicit or explicit contractual obligations attached to the receiving of gifts, even if some of these obligations, such as the pacification of potential troublemakers, might only be on an event-to-event basis. In his comparative study titled *The Gift,* Marcel Mauss (1924, pp. 1, 73) long ago realized that

> in theory gifts are voluntary, but in fact they are given and repaid under obligation. . . . Prestations which are in theory voluntary, disinterested and spontaneous, but are in fact obligatory and interested.

Kamenskii (1985, p. 48) made similar ethnographic observations. For Mauss, gift giving constituted an early form of contract and using wealth in this fashion was primarily a means of controlling others.

> The form usually taken is that of the gift generously offered; but the accompanying behaviour is formal pretense and social deception, while the transaction itself is based on obligation and economic self-interest. (Mauss 1924, p. 1)

If people periodically impoverished themselves by giving away all the wealth they could accumulate plus all the wealth they could borrow, it was only because they hoped to reap as many benefits as possible, and as quickly as possible, in the following phase of the reciprocal cycle. This behavior is similar to modern-day land investors who broker millions of dollars, but live in impoverished conditions because they spend all of their wealth and everything that they can borrow to invest in land they think will dramatically increase in value. Just as some of these land investors misjudge future markets and go bankrupt, so too, the aggrandizers in traditional transegalitarian societies must have periodically lost everything due to poor judgments and investments. This cultural ecological view is the one I have adopted in trying to understand prehistoric complex hunter–gatherers. It seems to work best (for further details see Hayden, 1995). If status and prestige play any role in systematic transegalitarian giving, they are probably euphemisms for success, wealth exchange "credit ratings," the ability to attract productive supporters, or reliable exchange partners, or to arrange advantageous marriages.

Aggrandizers also created or took advantage of pretexts for getting other community members to produce and surrender surplus. For instance, allies were needed to protect all the families in the community; losses suffered by allies had to be compensated for by payments of highly desired foods or wealth; peace had to be secured by exchanging wealth; good marriages could be obtained only by paying high prices to desirable families; children had to be properly trained and socially promoted to increase their worth in marriage; displays of food surplus and wealth were necessary to demonstrate the success and desirability of marrying into specific groups; the spirits had to be appeased for misfortunes and thanked for good fortunes, and so on. All these matters proved to be compelling pretexts that aggrandizers used to generate and get control of the surplus production capacities of their kin and community neighbors. Enhancing the value of children as part of these strategies was more common than usually acknowledged by archaeologists and seemed to result in the burial of children with ascribed prestige goods even though there might be no hereditary classes or formal chiefdoms.

Once some pretext or lure was accepted by others for producing and surrendering some of their surplus, aggrandizers maneuvered themselves into positions of control over the use of these resources by acting as feast organizers, war leaders, peace negotiators, parents with control over children's marriages, and as ritual experts. From these vantage points, they could appropriate some of the contributed surplus and labor for their own benefit and use legitimized expenses for the events or for compensation of their own efforts.

One form of compensation was undoubtedly the privileged use, if not outright stewardship or ownership, of community surplus. Control of surplus food or wealth could be demanded under the guise of needing them for special events that the community had agreed to sponsor, such as feasts for alliances. Initially, in order to draw as many community members into such schemes as possible (thereby maximizing the benefits for the aggrandizer or organizers), it would have been necessary to make the events as appealing and beneficial to other community members as possible. It would have been necessary to offer key support personnel more advantages. Similarly, many families were undoubtedly included in the initial establishment of owned corporate resources. A wide base of support in all these endeavors was necessary to prevent the special privileges sought by aggrandizers from collapsing under the weight of lethargy or counter-claims of the egalitarian majority of the community. More than anything else, these considerations probably explain the surprising proportion of communities that were considered "elites" in both the ethnographies and archaeological investigations, that is, from one-half to two-thirds of the community. Similar proportions seem to characterize both prehistoric and historic elites versus commoners on the Northwest Coast where half of the long houses were occupied by elite families (Chatters, 1989, pp. 176–177; Mitchell & Donald, 1985; Boelscher, 1989, p. 50; Ames, personal communication, 1995). And similar situations also characterize many transegalitarian societies in Southeast Asia with "hereditary" elites (Leach, 1954, pp. 149, 162–163, 214). In all these cases, elite probably refers to those families with an active claim to decision-making and benefits in corporate groups that owned valuable resources. Commoners were those without rights to valuable, privately owned resources or to participation in the decision making of the major corporate groups. Active aggrandizers provided the main aggressive energy for organizing corporate groups, feasts, and other events from which they could derive benefits. These individuals were recognized as the *real* elites, that is, as people who had validated their hereditary status. However, it is unlikely that all the individuals who were born into elite families were politically, economically, and socially aggressive. Many elite individuals were probably content to passively participate in the advantages and responsibilities that they inherited or, in the case of very lazy people, even to lapse into relative obscurity or poverty, retaining only the right to reactivate their claim to participate more fully in corporate affairs should they or their descendants become more ambitious and productive at a future date. Thus, it would be a mistake to view half of the communities, or even half of the large corporate groups, as being obsessively driven by social and economic advancement. Undoubtedly some were, but this number need not have been great for the system to have worked well. The proportion of aggressive, acquisitive, aggrandizing, triple-A personalities in the general population might be as low as 1 to 10%, which is probably not very different from the proportion of equivalent personality types in modern industrial societies.

If it seems that transegalitarian elites initially formed a large proportion of community populations, it also appears that as surplus production increased and the power of aggrandizers increased and was consolidated over time, the aggrandizers progressively excluded more and more people from elite status. In short, they began restructuring and minimizing the costs of running their support network wherever possible so that they could concentrate more benefits in their own hands and in the hands of those who they absolutely needed to make the system work. As a result, later chiefdoms and states probably had smaller proportions of elites than transegalitarian communities. For instance, Adams and Smith (1981, p. 346) argue that Classic Maya elites constituted only 1.5% of the population.

Thus, rather than elites emerging as a narrow, privileged group of people from the egalitarian ranks, it appears that elites became established by creating a broadly based privileged group with benefits widely shared. Only after such groups were created could aggrandizers then progressively let go of less useful or productive families without significant repercussions. The occurrence of productive resources in highly localized geographical areas, such as prime fishing locations, or prime agricultural land in the valley bottoms, or control over prime trade routes, probably helped aggrandizers concentrate their power in the form of corporate groups and narrow support bases, as suggested by Matson (1985) and Quilter (personal communication). However, these are issues best explored in subsequent readings (e.g., Hayden, 1995).

Feasts were important in most of the brokering of alliances, investments, and displays of success because they were both public and usually ritualistic in nature. Being public, they ensured that everyone present witnessed agreements between participants, the amounts given by one party to another, and the amounts therefore owed. Ritual gatherings were also used to solemnly bind those same agreements and exchanges, perhaps with the added threat of divine displeasure and consequent ill fortune if they should be broken. On the Plateau, pipe smoking was one such solemn ritual that bound individuals to honor their word and treat those who shared the pipe as allies. Pipes held enormous sacred power. Feasting contexts for these arrangements also provided a good opportunity for the hosts to show off their successes and to try to impress marriageable and other talented guests with the desirability or material advantages of being part of the hosts' economic and social consortium (chapter 2).

Aggrandizers not only promoted and presided over these feasts and the social/economic obligations that they entailed, but the aggrandizers also tried to organize the host group into as impressive dancing and ritual dramatic performances as possible. For feasts, aggrandizers tried to get host participants to obtain impressive costuming. They also tried to obtain impressive foods and serving vessels. Aggrandizers tried to procure rare, impressive, novel, and costly objects to give to guests and place them in the debt of a reciprocal exchange—for an unreciprocated formal gift in traditional societies was a declaration of hostility and potential warfare (see Mauss's book on this topic). Aggrandizers used all means at their disposal to impress, indebt, and create pressures to produce ever more surplus. Once a costly gift was given in public to a corporate group, all members had to contribute to its repayment or face losing allies, future marriage partners, credit, and self-respect. The consequences could be dire. Aggrandizers knew this and used this lever to get corporate and community members to surrender greater and greater amounts of surplus to the maximum extent that members permitted themselves to be pushed.

For gift giving, it was often necessary to obtain rare, flashy objects from distant sources. This aspect shows up particularly well in the archaeological record. At Keatley Creek, we have obsidian from Anaheim Lake, 350 km to the northwest; moose antler from Prince George, 400 km to the north; dentalium and other coastal shells from 300 km to the west; and cherts from Idaho. In fact, regional trade of prestige items is one of the hallmarks of complex hunter–gatherers and makes sense in terms of feasting activities meant to lure others into debt relationships. I suspect that the holding of slaves and many types of prestige technologies, such as metalworking, also originated as part of aggrandizers' schemes to impress allies, foes, and followers. Keatley Creek and the other large Lillooet villages were especially important in this trade since they occupied the most easily traversable valley corridors between the Interior and the Coast (see Figure 1.1). They could therefore exert great control over this trade and amass great profits like their compatriots at the Coastal ends of these corridors (Ferguson, 1984, pp. 286–287, 304, 314).

In communities with large residential corporate groups, such as the Classic Lillooet and Northwest Coast groups, feasts were generally held within the large houses of the hosts. However, private feasting and debt creation probably also took place between smaller groups of powerful elites in these communities as part of secret societies or similar organizations. Thus, it is likely that special, elite feasting structures may also be present at Keatley Creek. We have identified three structures that could have been used for special feasts, and we are now in the process of excavating them. However, there are other indications of feasting activities at the site. These include large outside roasting or cooking areas that seem to be associated with the largest houses and the probable ritual structures. Remains of dance and ritual paraphernalia, as well as an impressive dog ceremony noted in the last chapter, were also likely part of major feasts. Central parts of the floor in Housepit 7 are suspiciously devoid of artifacts and consist of a finer loam matrix than other areas of the floor, indicating possible use for sacred performances meant to impress onlookers.

Why should ambitious aggrandizers emerge only in the last 10,000 to 20,000 years or so in the world? I believe that both genetic variations and variations in early-life experiences have ensured that some aggrandizing personalities have always been present in human breeding populations. However, when resources were scarce or easily overexploitable or unreliable, sharing was essential for survival. The majority of people in all communities refused to recognize aggrandizing claims or tolerate attempts by aggrandizers to use resources for their own benefit. People in these situations refused to enter into contractual debts that involved the production or surrender of surplus. They refused to recognize claims of private property. It was only when technological improvements made the production of surpluses possible on a sustained basis in some areas of the world, and when most people felt assured of being able to obtain adequate food for themselves in normal times, that the rigid proscriptions on aggrandizing behavior became relaxed. Elizabeth Cashdan (1980) has documented the transformation from an egalitarian to a nonegalitarian type of society among the Bushmen over a remarkably short period of time. In this case the transformation was triggered by the introduction of new resources through pastoral herders and wage labor associated with the industrial state. This is another clear example of how basic resource conditions have a profound effect on the manner in which people structure their social and ideological world.

SUMMARY

We have chronicled the presence of considerable inequality within the Keatley Creek site and even within its larger residential corporate groups. The economic foundations and probably the reason for the existence of these corporate groups are tied to controlling lucrative salmon-producing sites and the substantial food surpluses these sites yielded. This not only makes logical sense, but it also is supported by the ethnography and by the archaeological finds at the site. The most powerful residential corporate groups were surprisingly stable, probably persisting over more than 1,400 years with very little apparent change. They thus constitute the longest persistence of specific corporate groups known to have existed anywhere in the world.

How did some aggrandizing individuals convince other members of the community to generate and surrender control over some food surpluses? I argue that aggrandizers manipulated the self-interest of other community members to their own advantage, much like the sharp businessmen and con artists of the modern world. Aggrandizers were forever dreaming up projects that would appeal to others and which required contributions of work and goods from others whom they could control. They always tried to hook people into supporting their schemes by promising attractive personal benefits or gains. Only after the contracts were set did the full nature of the relationship probably become evident, and no doubt, it frequently turned out that the aggrandizer obtained the net benefit while the indebted person worked much harder to fulfill the terms of the contract than they had anticipated. Thus, I favor the "lure" explanation for the development of complexity.

Feasts were almost certainly an integral part of the strategies used by aggrandizers to attract supporters and to create debts. In their most developed forms, they functioned like modern banks requiring repayment plus an increment (interest) for all items given out. In fact, we can perceive many of the characteristics of modern, family-owned corporations or financial institutions in the corporate groups at Keatley Creek and among other complex hunter–gatherers. In essence, the elites of corporate groups were like our own corporate board members holding varying amounts of stock. These holdings in both cases were frequently inherited and could increase or decrease depending on how much work a family invested in the corporation and how much effort they put into making the corporate group successful. In both cases, individuals who wasted their resources because of laziness, excessive spending, gambling, or other poor judgments might find themselves divested of their privileges. Common tenant families of the corporate groups were like the working employees of modern companies, except that a thousand years ago in the Northwest, the management–owners and the workers lived together in the same large corporate house. Part-time workers probably lived in other smaller houses in the same neighborhood. And, just as modern financial institutions charge different interest rates on loans according to levels of economic success and risk, so the traditional, native corporate groups charged varying amounts of interest on loans, or gifts, according to the borrowers success and status in other economic ventures (Codere, 1950, p. 70). Thus, the origin of our type of society and economic institutions can be found in the emergence of complex hunter–gatherers. While evidence for feasting has been relatively neglected by archaeologists, it is becoming apparent that feasting may have played a pivotal role in the emergence of complex hunting and gathering societies, as well as in the initial development of complexity among horticultural societies. There is reasonably good evidence for feasting, too, at Keatley Creek, and we are now looking for more evidence.

I would like to emphasize that in order to undertake these and the many other types of investigations into the social, economic, and political organization of past cultures, it is absolutely essential to have intact, undisturbed sites to study. Today, most national, state, or provincial governments recognize the importance of archaeological sites for understanding our common and specific human heritages. These government bodies have enacted strict laws to protect archaeological sites. In effect, they view the unauthorized digging in sites and any removal of objects from sites as just as destructive as taking shotguns to rock art sites. Any of these activities are purely and simply destruction of people's heritage. At Keatley Creek, some destruction of the site has occurred, but we have been lucky that it has been relatively limited. Otherwise, this book could not have been written. No subsequent destruction of the site has occurred while we have worked there. Other sites have been far less fortunate. The destruction of archaeological sites today is one of the most critical problems facing our human heritage and the discipline of archaeology.

In the course of the preceding analyses, we have seen numerous instances where the basic nature of food resources has had a very strong effect on how humans behave and constitute their societies. At a general level, scarcity versus abundance has affected sharing, private ownership, the amount of economically based competition, the ability to amass and utilize surplus for individual benefits, and the development of prestige technologies. On a specific level, the periodic availability and value of resources, and the need for labor to generate wealth, exerted strong pressures for the formation of hierarchical corporate groups and polygynous marriages. Can you extend this approach by thinking of ways that the nature of the energy resources in contemporary societies have shaped the general and specific social institutions and cultural values that you are familiar with?

CHAPTER 9

Turning of the Sun
at Coyote's Great House

Keatley Creek is an arid place much of the year. Wind devils envelop sagebrush and prickly pear cacti in sudden gusts of dust without warning. The sun beats down on the backs of excavators squinting to distinguish natural rocks from encrusted artifacts. In the field, it is difficult to imagine flesh-and-blood people having held the dirt-caked artifacts that today are exposed to the light of day for the first time in one or two thousand years. It is hard to imagine the small fragments of animal bones with the flesh and fur that was once on them. It is hard to imagine the housepits filled with people and food, furs and feasting. Yet we now know that they were there. Sometimes on moonlit walks in the remains of the houses, it is a little easier to imagine these things.

Back in the laboratory, the careful inspection and recording of thousands of pieces of bone, stone, and charred plants does not lend itself to a view of what the living culture was like either. Each specialist works on a single part of the prehistoric puzzle, sometimes never knowing what lies beyond a pile of stone or bone. I have strived for interdisciplinary interaction in analyzing the archaeological remains from Keatley Creek, but this is not always easy to achieve. In an attempt to bring together the various threads and to breathe some life into the remains over which we have labored for 10 years, I would like readers to indulge me for a few more pages. I would like to present a glimpse of life in one of the great houses in the way I imagine it. Some of the details are based on the well-documented conclusions that have been discussed in preceding chapters. Some details are drawn from ethnographic observations on traditional Plateau life. Some details are based on my own hunches concerning what probably transpired and why (see Hayden, n.d., for further details). So, take this opportunity to relax and imagine that you are one of the guests that has been invited to Coyote's Great House, Housepit 7. The year is A.D. 950.

MOON OF THE TURNING SUN

The winter winds funneled through the frozen canyon, over the raging crests of the great river, whistling above the creek like the bone flutes that pubescent girls played when alone in their special huts. Although the hunter's family was not of noble lineage, they had agreed to help support Coyote's Great House in the upcoming feast to celebrate the Turning of the Sun, the Winter Solstice. The hunter had uncommon luck during the fall, killing two deer during the season. His wife had dried half the meat and spent many hours turning the hides into a buckskin shirt, a quiver, moccasin boots, and some other small items. It was above all the dried deer meat that the nobles in Coyote's House were interested in procuring for distribution to their guests. They had agreed to repay the hunter with dried salmon and a flawed, heavily used nephrite adze after the next Salmon Moon, more than a half a year away.

The repayment was not nearly everything the hunter had hoped for. If anything, it seemed somewhat less than equitable. However, the cousin of the Firstman in Coyote's House had assured the hunter that he and his immediate family would be welcome to attend the Turning of the Sun feast at Coyote's Great House. Moreover, the hunter had always yearned to own a nephrite adze, and this might be one of the few opportunities to acquire one, even if it was not of very good quality. He also secretly hoped that members of the Coyote House would be sufficiently impressed with his abilities as a hunter and his willingness to work hard so that they might consider enlisting him and his family as one of the non-noble families of the Great House. His wife was a great asset for these hopes since she was known as a hard worker who produced some of the best dried meat in the region, meat that was neither completely hard and carbonized nor soft or rancid. It was always perfectly prepared and perfectly delicious. She was also renowned for making fine buckskin and clothing.

Being part of the Great House would mean more security from famine when the salmon failed to appear, for the great houses had more stored food than others. It would mean more security from attack when in the mountains, for the members of the great houses kept together in groups within their special mountain areas; it would also mean easier and less costly use of special items that had to be borrowed for special events, potential support for advancing further in occupations such as hunting, and potential support for arranging beneficial marriages for his children and advancing them in rank. And, finally, it would mean being able to participate in feasts more frequently than he could at present.

Therefore, tonight, it was essential to look and act as distinguished as possible. He wore his new buckskin shirt with its modest fringes. He and his wife borrowed other buckskin clothes and some simple bone jewelry from distant relatives, although there was a price to pay for borrowing these items. He had to give those families several pieces of the salmon that he was supposed to receive as repayment for his dried meat. His two children put on their sagebark shirts that were made that autumn and then wrapped themselves in small robes of dog skins sewed together. The robes were from vagrant dogs that no one had fed or cared for, dogs that would have died that winter from starvation.

When they had painted their faces by the light of birch bark candles, and combed and oiled their hair, when everyone was ready, they opened the side-door flap and ventured into the bitter cold, leaving a scant, smouldering fire in the house for the other three families that remained behind. Their house was small, but usually snug and warm enough with 18 people in close quarters. Outside, the wind rattled the high, boney branches of the cottonwoods in the creekbed and the children clung to their parents, fearing the cannibal spirits that were reported to roam the country on nights like this. The stars were like thousands of piercing spectral eyes. This was the night that the sun would turn in its path according to Coyote's sacred men, the men who daily recorded the setting position of the sun from behind certain trees (Teit, 1900, p. 239; 1909, pp. 604, 610). The feasting and gaming had already begun two days ago; however, only a few select noble families had been invited for those first days. This was to be the most important night of feasting.

The hunter and his family did not have far to go and could already see the long ladder pole with the Coyote sculptured high on its end, eerily illuminated from the bright fires underneath the smoke hole. The entrance cover had been removed for this event in order to allow the smoke to escape and to cool off the dense crowd of spectators. As the hunter and his family approached the base of Coyote's Great House, they passed five long poles stuck into the ground, pointing skyward, each with the partly decomposed and frozen body of a sacrificed dog at its end, the muzzles pointing skyward. These were messengers to Coyote and other spirits, bearing requests for abundant deer and salmon, for fertile marriages, and for the wealth exchanges that accompanied good marriages. Only the skulls remained on the poles from the dogs sacrificed in previous years. In the winter skies, beneath the sacrificial poles and the strangely lit Coyote ladder, there was certainly the feeling that Coyote himself was present and hovering around the entrance.

They walked on the mats, spread with sweet-smelling fir boughs, covering the path leading up to the great ladder (Teit, 1912b, p. 367). The path passed by the covered and steaming roasting pit just beyond the edge of the house. Delicious smells steamed up from the earth and provided mouthwatering portents of the meal to come. The hunter and his family began their ascent on the roof path. They peered in through the entrance hole vibrating with the sound of drums being played in unison, sounds focused through the entrance like an acoustic funnel. It was almost like looking underground at a light- and sound-filled spectacle, obstructed in part by a platform of poles halfway down. One by one, the hunter and his family descended the ladder to the platform and then continued on another ladder to the bustling floor where one of the House workers greeted them and escorted them to a mat and evergreen-covered part of the floor among the common families of the great house. All the mats and hammocks that usually hung between the large support posts had been taken down for the feast (Condrashoff, 1980, p. 5).

The hunter and his wife gazed around in wonder at the sumptuous display, the likes of which they had never seen. The most impressive scene was the Firstman and his entourage, for he was seated on a wall bench richly covered with deer and bear furs, behind which were elaborately decorated mat hangings bearing the stylized face of Coyote together with symbols of the places where he performed his magical feats. The Firstman wore long-fringed buckskin pants and shirt, embroidered with various colored porcupine quills and trimmed in places with lynx and fox furs. His headdress was full of eagle feathers, other colored feathers, and was trimmed with fur (Figure 9.1). Sparkling white dentalium shells and glittering copper beads and squares covered his chest; a long nephrite adze hung from his belt. Red and white paint accentuated his imposing noble features. His three wives sat on either side, with his first wife similarly arrayed in the finest white-fringed buckskin decorated with many dentalium shells and much quillwork. The women's glistening hair was made even more beautiful by the white bone combs and pins ornately carved and then set into their coiffures. By their sides sat their children, all finely dressed in

FIGURE 9.1. *These are some of the finest traditional clothes of the Interior Salish Indians of British Columbia. All these garments are made of the finest, most supple buckskin and are handsomely beaded. They are worthy of the most wealthy and powerful traditional families and represent their attire for special events. The man on the left also wears a fine headdress of rare feathers. The woman at right has a lavish display of costly fringing on many of her garments, as well as fur on her cape.*

buckskin clothes. Beneath the Firstman sat two male slaves almost completely naked and shorn of their hair. To the left, his female slave was occupied together with the House's common women in preparing food for the coming feast. There were large piles of dried meat, berry cakes, and skin bottles containing salmon oil (Bishop, 1987, p. 77). The Firstman's most valuable hunting dog had also been brought into the house for this special occasion and lay by the slaves. His pet fox was attached to one of the platform posts. The scene was so awe-inspiring that the hunter did not dare look directly at these nobles.

Instead, he gazed straight ahead at the other noble families of the house, all arrayed against the opposite wall, and all lavishly dressed but in a slightly less grandiose manner than the Firstman. They, too, had beautifully decorated mat hangings, baskets, buckskin clothes, and jewelry. There was much more movement among the other noble families as they played the spiritually powerful drums, rattles, and whistles of the House. They then began singing and preparing for the dances. The Coyote dancers all wore impressive costumes and jewelry, with their faces painted to resemble coyote features. They howled as they began dancing in the special sacred area in front of the Firstman. One of the dancers wore the special ancestral Coyote mask of the House. The dentalium shells that adorned their shirts were only loosely attached so that a number of shells fell off as they swayed to and fro during the dance. Everyone watched the shells fall to the floor with eyes wide while the less inhibited children darted into the dance area to pick them up (Teit, 1912b, pp. 358–359).

Each noble family had a blazing fire in front of their seats in the house. The invited noble guests sat on mats opposite from their hosts, as well as in the available parts of the center floor. The hunter and other guests of lower status sat tightly packed with the House workers behind the guest nobles. Behind them all, children scampered up on the wall slope of the house and crouched under the roof in order to see better. Other children perched themselves on the entrance landing to watch the events below.

After over two hours of drumming, singing, and dancing almost everyone had arrived and the more formal parts of the feasting events began. Between the heat of the fires and the heat generated by the energetic drummers and the 150 people crowded inside the house, the hunter began to feel uncomfortably warm, and he wondered how the Firstman could tolerate the heat with all of the buckskin clothes and furs that he was wearing.

The Firstman finally beckoned to his spokesman who conveyed instructions to the dancers to end. At a signal from one of the drummers, all of the drumming and dancing came to a sudden stop. The Firstman waited and then rose from his seat and walked in a stately fashion to the center of the floor in front of his seat. His spokesman servant held up his arms for silence. When there was silence, the Firstman began speaking in the special language that nobles used amongst themselves. The hunter could only guess at the general meanings of some of the words. The Firstman's mouthpiece addressed the guests, translating and welcoming them on behalf of the Firstman and the entire Great House of Coyote. He expounded upon the spiritual strength of Coyote, the ancestral founder of the Great House who lived many scores of generations ago before the great transformations that occurred throughout the land. The Firstman expounded upon the continuing good training and upbringing of all Coyote's descendants. He expounded upon the great rewards that had been given to Coyote's descendants for their trueness of spirit, for their spiritual training, and for their diligent work. They were a great house, one of the most powerful of all the land. Their wealth and success was proof of their spiritual worth. They brought valuable shells from the coast; they brought furs and robes from the great houses to the east; they brought slaves and sun metal; they brought sparkling black arrowstone from the distant north; they married their daughters to great and wealthy families of the Coast; no one dared attack their members whether in their homeland or elsewhere; they traveled far to the southern great river and returned with wonderous tales and powerful carved objects. Tonight, Coyote's Great House would elevate three of their most meritorious children to greater status and worth so that they could continue the noble tradition that Coyote had begun. The Firstman spoke at great length of all these matters and the valuable characteristics of the children being elevated. His words resonated from the conical roof and came back to his ears in a focused, amplified, almost echoic fashion that seemed to give a magical quality to his words, although only he could hear this effect since only he was at the center of the house floor.

Finally, after going on about all these matters, the Firstman drew to a close, once more welcoming his noble guests and inviting them to share his pipe, to receive his food, and to receive the wealth of Coyote. His mouthpiece servant brought the Firstman his pipe pouch and lit the pipe for him, a pipe full of sacred herbs from the mountains that relaxed the smokers and enhanced their enjoyment of the drumming, dancing, and feasting. The Firstman took the first puffs and then passed it to the next highest ranking noble in the house. It was passed successively to the next highest ranking persons until all the Coyote noblemen and invited nobles had partaken of the sacred ritual. The house workers then busied themselves in serving salmon bone and lily root soups, smoke-dried deer meat, the best fillets of dried chinook salmon, pieces of deer backfat, salmon oil to dip dried meats in, pounded salmon flour mixed with oil and dried berries, melted deer grease, dried Saskatoon and other berries, and lily roots roasted in the earth oven outside. The nobles ate their fill of the best of all these delicious servings in carefully made bowls and trays of birch bark. Afterward, the non-noble guests were served the more common pink or sockeye salmon and smaller portions of dried meat and soup. Water was provided liberally in birch bark cups to all who requested it.

In an hour or so, as the feasting began to subside, the Firstman and his mouthpiece servant once again stood at the center of the house to address the guests. He once again expounded the virtues of the Great House and the necessity of proper upbringing of children to carry on the traditions and the success of the house. Without spiritual and physical training, no proper or beneficial marriages were possible. No success in any occupation could be attained. Therefore, the nobles of the house had trained and paid for the proper education of the three children being honored this night. Tonight, two of them were to receive a second piercing of their ears and one was to receive several tattoo marks. Dressed in especially handsome fringed white buckskin clothes, the children were presented to the entire assembly. They were then led to the sacred men and women of the house where the piercing and tattooing operations took place during the next hour using special sharpened bone awls. When this was done, the now elevated children were presented once again to the crowd, and they were given valuable gifts of dentalium shells, packages of dried meat, dressed deer skins, and eagle feathers. Similar presents were given to noble guests who were considered as potential providers of marriage partners for the children and as close allies of Coyote's House. Lesser gifts such as bark cups and decorative feathers were given to other supportive families. The value of all the presents distributed was a measure of the increased worth of the children.

The Firstman again called for silence. He announced a surprise special event in honor of the richness that the House had accumulated that year, in honor of the children being elevated, and in honor of the guests that were being repaid for their

previous gifts. In order to make the ceremony even more spectacular than expected, the Great House had paid the Wolf Dance society to perform its renowned Wolf
Dance ceremony. His mouthpiece servant used a bone whistle to signal the beginning of the event. The drumming and singing began at once with a vigorous
rhythm. Whistles made the air bristle.

Unexpectedly, five young men with blackened faces jumped down from the
entrance landing to the floor. They wore only loincloths and their appearance was
wild. They danced in a frenetic fashion to the rapid drumbeats. Their looks became
more and more strained as they whirled and jumped in movements that seemed to
defy normal physical possibilities. After dancing for some time nearly to exhaustion, one of the men put on a wolf skin and immediately began to act like a wolf,
snapping at guests and even biting some of them and drawing their blood. Several
other men brought in a packdog that was no longer very useful. The wolf dancers
seized the dog, which began howling as they danced with it, and began pulling its
legs and throwing it in the air or flinging it to the ground. The drumming became
louder and louder. At the climax of the dance the main wolf dancer began to bite the
legs of the dog and froth at the mouth until he was in such a state of frenzy that he
strangled the dog with his bare hands and bit into the dog's flesh, tearing pieces off
and eating them. He ferociously disemboweled the dog with a stone knife. The
dance continued for a few minutes longer, until a Coyote sacred man finally stepped
forward with his sacred magical staff crowned by the sun and held it up above
the dancers (Teit, 1898, pp. 81, 93, 110, 261fn; 1912a, pp. 207, 312). He called to
the coyote dancers and touched them with his staff, one by one. As he did this, the
drumming subsided and the dancers became calmer although the main dancer was
having difficulty calming himself and never stopped his jerky spasms. The sacred
man then led them away through the smoke hole to another house where they would
be purified for several days and would recover from their ordeal.

Amidst the excited chatter of the guests, the Firstman stepped forward again
and thanked the noble guests for their past gifts and for inviting the Coyote House
to previous feasts. The Firstman stated that Coyote's Great House always paid its
debts and was without shame or dishonor. Coyote's House held vast resources along
the Great River and in the mountains. It was wealthy with powerful leaders, fertile
women, and productive workers. Therefore, they would not merely return what had
been given to them in years past, but they would augment the value of those gifts by
a third again of their value. While Bear House had given Coyote House 10 strings
of dentalium shells at the Sun's Turning five winters ago, Coyote House was now
giving them 13 strings of dentalium shells. And the Firstman motioned his slaves to
display the strings of shells to all the guests and to present them to the Firstman of
Bear House (Teit, 1912a, p. 384). The Coyote Firstman took several puffs from the
sacred pipe and gestured to the skies. His servant transferred the pipe to the Bear
Firstman who also took several puffs and made similar gestures. This sealed a pact
between them with a sacred vow. The members of Bear House were now obligated
to return at least an equal amount of wealth at a future feast.

While Frog House had given three suits of fine buckskin clothes and three long
nephrite adzes to Coyote House at the Sun's Turning seven winters ago, they would
now receive four suits of new buckskin clothes and three long nephrite adzes, plus

a shorter one. They, too, shared the sacred pipe. And so the distribution of wealth continued for over an hour until all the debts had been paid, the increases duly noted by all present and committed to memory by the special recallers of the House. During the public distribution of wealth, the hearts of the members of Coyote House filled with pride as well as eager expectations for even greater returns of wealth in the years to come.

After this lavish distribution of wealth, the drumming, singing, and dancing resumed. The nobles began playing lahal, the "bone game" of cunning, chance, and spiritual knowledge in which much wealth could be won or lost including valuable buckskin clothes and even one's wives, children, or one's own freedom (Teit, 1912a, p. 375; 1912b, pp. 338–339). The Coyote team played against other teams far into the night and into the next day. Coyote's Firstman experienced one of the most intense feelings of power and spiritual exaltation that he was ever to know in his entire lifetime. He would strive for years to try to achieve another comparable experience: the magical sound of his words; the hushed silence and attention of everyone; the entrancing drumming, singing, and dancing; the expansive feeling of power and prestige. All this made the years of preparation, work, and headaches worthwhile. Once he had experienced this intense elation, he could never stop his involvement (Polly Wiessner, personal communication). Besides, even if he wanted to, he could not. He owed far too much to all the people that he had borrowed from in order to give away all the wealth distributed at this feast. He had to pay them back or he would have to declare himself bankrupt and be reduced to rubbish status. Irate creditors might even try to kill him. He could never get out of the obligations into which he and the rest of Coyote's House had entered. It was an endless sequence of exchanges that he was passing on to his children. Only death would ultimately deliver him from the vicious cycle, the pressures, and the headaches that accompanied these reciprocal and competitive feasts.

EPILOGUE

After another day of dancing, feasting, distributing minor gifts, and playing lahal, the feast at Coyote's Great House ended. On the last day of the feast, a sacred man of the house collected all of the sacrificed dog remains from the poles and the ground underneath the poles. He placed these and the body of the packdog that had been sacrificed in the Wolf Dance ceremony in one of the storage pits within the house that had been emptied of its salmon and roots for the feast. He buried the dog bones and bodies in that pit. Being present under the living floor, the bones would forever be messengers to the spirits on behalf of Coyote's Great House. The nobles and supporters of the House would not hold another such feast for eight more years, for it took that long to accumulate enough wealth for a great feast. In the intervening years, they would be guests at repayment feasts held by other great houses and some of the lesser houses in their turns.

The hunter and his family envied the nobles of Coyote's Great House for their wealth, power, and high status. He continued to be successful in hunting and would be invited to become part of the workforce of Coyote's House five winters later when there was a vacant common hearth in the house. His children would eventually be elevated to near noble status and sponsored in marriage by the Great House.

However, only three generations later an unexpected catastrophe struck the entire region. Everyone had felt the ground shake, and the roofs of several old houses had even partially collapsed. No one had suspected that the shaking had broken off the entire side of a mountain that came crashing down into the Great River two days' walk downstream from their winter village at the place shown in Figure 1.3. It was thus two days before they learned of the catastrophe. The landslide had dammed the Great River almost completely, creating a huge lake behind it. For days, the riverbed below the landslide was dry as the lake filled up. Then the water topped the dam and continued flowing; but in the late summer of that year only a few of the most powerful chinook salmon managed to swim up the falls created by the slide. None of the scores of millions of sockeye and pink salmon could swim past the landslide dam (see Hayden & Ryder, 1991).

The once lucrative fishing sites that provided wealth and nourishment for the Classic Lillooet communities had become barren. The people used up all of their stored foods. They exchanged their wealth for food from distant bands. Many people began to starve that year. The following years were no better. The dam held for almost a generation. By the time that it was finally worn down by the river, the cycle of salmon returning to spawn in the fresh streams and lakes above Lillooet had been completely broken. It would take centuries for the fabulous salmon runs to become reestablished above the landslide.

In the meantime, the occupants of once mighty villages, the most sophisticated and complex villages of the northern Plateau, had abandoned their homeland to live with families allied to them through exchange and marriage. The poor had no allies to fall back upon, nowhere to go, and no food left to procure. Many of them perished from starvation. The hunter and his wife, as well as the Coyote Firstman who organized the memorable feast, had all died before the great catastrophe. Only their great-grandchildren were left to pick up the broken pieces of their long heritage and continue on as best as possible, one day hoping to reestablish the greatness of their ancestors when abundant resources were again part of their domain.

Winter Solstice
Vancouver 1994

REFERENCES

Adams, R. E. W., & Smith, W. (1981). Feudal models for Classic Maya civilization. In W. Ashmore (Ed.), *Lowland Maya settlement patterns* (pp. 335–350). Albuquerque: University of New Mexico Press.

Adams, R. McC., & Nissen, H. (1972). *The Uruk countryside.* Chicago: University of Chicago Press.

Albright, S. (1984). *Tahltan Ethnoarchaeology.* (Publication No. 15). Burnaby, BC: Simon Fraser University, Archaeology Department.

Arnold, J. (1996). The archaeology of complex hunter(gatherers. *Journal of Archaeological Method and Theory, 3,* 77–126.

Beaton, J. M. (1991). Extensification and intensification in central California prehistory. *Antiquity, 65,* 946–952.

Berry, K. (1991). Prehistoric salmon utilization at the Keatley Creek site. Paper presented at the 44th annual Northwest Anthropological meetings, Missoula, MT.

Bettinger, R. (1978). Alternative adaptive strategies in the prehistoric Great Basin. *Journal of Anthropological Research, 34,* 27–46.

Bettinger, R. (1983). Aboriginal sociopolitical organization in Owens Valley: Beyond the family band. In E. Tooker & M. Fried (Eds), *The development of political organization in native North America.* (pp. 45–58). Washington, DC: American Ethnological Society.

Binford, L. (1973). Interassemblage variability—the Mousterian and the "functional" argument. In C. Renfrew (Ed.), *The explanation of culture change: Models in prehistory* (pp. 227–254). Pittsburgh: University of Pittsburgh Press.

Birdsell, J. (1972). *Human evolution.* Chicago: Rand McNally and Co.

Bishop, C. (1987). Coast–interior exchange: The origins of stratification in northwestern North America. *Arctic Anthropology, 24,* 72–83.

Boelscher, M. (1989). *The curtin within: Haida social and mythological discourse.* Vancouver: University of British Columbia Press.

Carneiro, R. (1967). On the relationship between size of population and complexity of social organization. *Southwestern Journal of Anthropology, 23,* 234–243.

Cashdan, E. (1980). Egalitarianism among hunters and gatherers. *American Anthropologist, 82,* 116–120.

Chatters, J. (1989). The antiquity of economic differentiation within households in the Puget Sound region, Northwest Coast. In S. MacEachern, D. Archer, & R. Garvin (Eds.), *Households and communities* (pp. 168–178). Calgary: Archaeological Association of the University of Calgary.

Clark, J., & Blake, M. (1989). The emergence of rank societies on the Pacific Coasts of Chiapas, Mexico. Paper presented at the Circum-Pacific Prehistory Conference, Seattle, WA.

Clark, J., & Parry, W. (1990). Craft specialization and cultural complexity. *Research in Economic Anthropology, 12,* 289–346.

Codere, H. (1950). *Fighting with property.* Seattle: University of Washington Press.

Condrashoff, N. (1972). *Edited transcript of interview with Shuswap informant, Isaac Willard: September, 1972, Shuswap Lake, BC.* Unpublished manuscript on file at the Royal British Columbia Museum, Victoria, British Columbia.

Condrashoff, N. (1980). *The pithouse.* Manuscript on file at the Royal British Columbia Museum, Victoria, British Columbia.

Darwent, J. (1996). *The prehistoric use of nephrite on the British Columbia Plateau.* Master's thesis, Simon Fraser University, Burnaby, British Columbia.

Dawson, G. (1892). Notes on the Shuswap people of British Columbia. *Proceedings and Transactions of the Royal Society of Canada, 9,* (2), 3–44.

Donald, L., (1985). On the possibility of social class in societies based on extractive subsistence. In M. Thompson, M. Garcia, & F. Kense (Eds.), *Status, structure, and stratification* (pp. 237–243). Calgary: Archaeological Association of the University of Calgary.

Donald, L., & Mitchell, D. (1975). Some correlates of local group rank among the southern Kwakiutl. *Ethnology, 14,* 325–346.

Dumond, D., & Minor, R. (1983). The Wildcat Canyon site. *Anthropological Papers, 30,* Eugene, OR.

Feil, D. K. (1987). *The evolution of Highland Papua New Guinea societies.* Cambridge: Cambridge University Press.

Ferguson, R. B. (1984). A reexamination of the causes of Northwest Coast warfare. In R. Ferguson (Ed.), *Warfare, culture, and environment* (pp. 267–328). New York: Academic Press.

Fladmark, K. (1982). Microdebitage analysis: initial considerations. *Journal of Archaeological Science, 9,* 205–220.

Garfield, V. (1966). The Tsimshian and their neighbors. In V. Garfield & P. Wingert (Eds.), *The Tsimshian Indians and their arts.* Seattle: University of Washington.

Goldman, I. (1940). The Alkatcho Carrier of British Columbia. In R. Linton (Ed.), *Acculturation in seven American Indian tribes* (pp. 333–386). New York: Appleton-Century-Crofts.

Gould, R., & Saggers, S. (1985). Lithic procurement in Central Australia: A closer look at Binford's idea of embeddedness in archaeology. *American Antiquity, 50,* 117–136.

Gould, S. J. (1987). Wonderful life: Tahe Burgess Shale and the nature of history. New York: W. W. Norton.

Grosse, E. (1896). *Die formen der familie und die formen der wirtschaft.* Freiburg, Leipzig: Mohr.

Harris, M. (1985). *Culture, people, nature.* New York: Harper and Row.

Hayden, B. (1975). Dingoes: pets or producers? *Mankind, 10,* 11–15.

Hayden, B. (1977). Corporate groups and the Late Ontario Iroquoian longhouse. *Ontario Archaeology, 28,* 3–16

Hayden, B. (1992). Conclusions: Ecology and complex hunter–gatherers. In B. Hayden (Ed.), *A complex culture of the British Columbia Plateau: Stl'atl'imx resource use* (pp. 525–564). Vancouver: University of British Columbia Press.

Hayden, B. (1995). Pathways to power: Principles for creating socioeconomic inequalities. In T. D. Price & G. Feinman (Eds.), *Foundations of social inequality* (pp. 15–85). New York: Plenum Press.

Hayden, B. (1996). Thresholds of power in emergent complex societies. In J. Arnold (Ed.), Emergent complexity: The evolution of intermediate societies, *International Monographs in Prehistory,* Ann Arbor, MI.

Hayden, B., Bakewell, E., & Gargett, R. (1996). The world's longest-lived corporate group: Lithic sourcing reveals prehistoric social organization near Lillooet, British Columbia. *American Antiquity, 61,* 341–356.

Hayden, B., n.d. *Final report of the excavations at Keatley Creek 1986–1995.* Manuscript on file with the British Columbia Provincial Archaeology Branch, Victoria, British Columbia.

Hayden, B., & Cannon, A. (1982). The corporate group as an archaeological unit. *Journal of Anthropological Archaeology, 1,* 132–158.

Hayden, B., & Ryder, J. (1991). Prehistoric cultural collapse in the Lillooet area. *American Antiquity, 56,* 50–65.

Helms, M. (1994). Chiefdom rivalries, control, and external contacts in lower Central America. In E. Brumfiel & J. Fox (Eds.), *Factional competition and political development in the New World* (pp. 55–60). Cambridge: Cambridge University Press.

Huelsbeck, D. (1994). Mammals and fish in the subsistence economy of Ozette. In S. Samuels (Ed.), *Ozette Archaelological Project research report, 2: Fauna* (pp. 17–92). Reports of investigations, 66: Pullman and National Park Service. Seattle, Washington State University Anthropology Department.

Jewitt, J. (Smith, D., Ed.), (1974). *The adventures and sufferings of John R. Jewitt, captive among the Nootka, 1803–1805.* Toronto: McClelland and Stewart.

Junker, L., Mudar, K., & Schwaller, M. (1994). Social stratification, household wealth, and competitive feasting in 15th/16th-century Philippine chiefdoms. *Research in Economic Anthropology, 15,* 307–358.

Kamenski, A. (1985). *Tlingit Indians of Alaska.* Fairbanks: University of Alaska Press.

Kennedy, D. & Bouchard, R. (1992). Stl'atl'imx (Fraser River Lillooet) fishing. In B. Hayden (Ed.), *A complex culture of the British Columbia Plateau* (pp. 266–354). Vancouver: University of British Columbia Press.

Kerber, J. (1997). *Lambert Farm: Public archaeology and canine burials along Narragansett Bay.* Fort Worth: Harcourt Brace.

Kim, S. (1994). Burials, pigs, and political prestige in Neolithic China. *Current Anthropology, 35,* 119–141.

Langemann, E. G. (1987). *Zooarchaeology of the Lillooet region, British Columbia.* Master's thesis, Simon Fraser University, Archaeology Department, Burnaby, British Columbia.

Leach, E. R. (1954). *Political systems of highland Burma.* Boston: Beacon Press.

Lepofsky, D., Kusmer, K., Hayden, B., & Lertzman, K. (1995). Reconstructing prehistoric socioeconomies from paleoethnobotanical and zooarchaeological data: An example from the British Columbia Plateau. *Journal of Ethnobiology, 16,* 31–62.

Matson, R. G. (1985). The relationship between sedentism and status inequalities among hunters and gatherers. In M. Thompson, M. T. Garcia, & F. Kense (Eds.), *Status, structure and stratification.* (pp. 245–252). Calgary: Archaeological Association of the University of Calgary.

Mauss, M. (1924). *The gift.* (Translation, 1954) New York: Free Press.

Mitchell, D., & Donald, L. (1985). Some economic aspects of Tlingit, Haida, and Tsimshian slavery. *Research in Economic Anthropology, 7,* 19–35.

Morgan, L. H. (1881). *Houses and house life of the American Aborigines.* Washington, DC: U.S. Geological Survey, Contributions to North American Ethnology, *IV.*

Naroll, R. (1956). A preliminary index of social development. *American Anthropologist, 58,* 687–715.

Oberg, K. (1973). *The social organization of the Tlingit Indians.* Seattle: University of Washington Press.

Plog, S. (1980). *Stylistic variation in prehistoric ceramics.* Cambridge: Cambridge University Press.

Price, D., & Brown, J. (Eds.). (1985). *Prehistoric hunter–gatherers.* Orlando, FL: Academic Press.

Randsborg, K. (1982). Rank, rights and resources: An archaeological perspective from Denmark. In C. Renfrew & S. Shennan (Eds.), *Ranking, resource and exchange* (pp. 132–140). Cambridge: Cambridge University Press.

Richards, T., & Rousseau, M. (1987). *Late prehistoric cultural horizons on the Canadian Plateau.* (Publication No. 16). Burnaby, BC: Simon Fraser University, Archaeology Department.

Romanoff, S. (21992a). Fraser Lillooet salmon fishing. In B. Hayden (Ed.), *A complex culture of the British Columbia Plateau* (pp. 222–265). Vancouver: University of British Columbia Press.

Romanoff, S. (1992b). The cultural ecology of hunting and potlatches among the Lillooet Indians. In B. Hayden (Ed.), *A complex culture of the British Columbia Plateau* (pp. 470–505). Vancouver: University of British Columbia Press.

Ryder, J. (1978). Geomorphology and late Quaternary history of the Lillooet area. In A. Stryd & S. Lawhead (Eds.), *Reports of the Lillooet archaeological project. no. 1: Introduction and setting* (pp. 56–57). Ottawa: National Museum of Man. (Mercury Series No. 73)

Samuels, S. (1991). Patterns in Ozette floor middens: Reflections of social units. In S. Samuels (Ed.), *Ozette archaeological project research reports: Vol. 1: House structure and floor midden* (pp. 175–270). Pullman, WA: Washington State University, Department of Anthropology. (Reports of Investigations, 63)

Scheffel, D. (1994). *We are the Shuswap: Reflections on the self-presentation of a B.C. first nation.* Paper presented at the 1994 BC Studies Conference, Kelowna, British Columbia.

Schiffer, M. (1987). *Formation processes of the archaeological record.* Albuquerque: University of New Mexico Press.

Schulting, R. (1995). *Mortuary variability and status differentiation on the Columbia-Fraser Plateau.* Burnaby, BC: Archaeology Press, Simon Fraser University.

Shnirelman, V. (1992). Complex hunter–gatherers: Exception or common phenomenon? *Dialectical Anthropology, 17,* 183–96.

Spafford, J. (1991). *Artifact distribution on floors and social organization in housepits at the Keatley Creek site.* Unpublished master's thesis, Simon Fraser University, Archaeology Department, Burnaby, British Columbia.

Stanislawski, M. (1973). Review of "Archaeology as anthropology: A case study." *American Antiquity, 38,* 117–122.

Stanislawski, M. (1974). The relationships of ethnoarchaeology, traditional and systems archaeology. In C. Donnan & C. Clewlow (Eds.), *Ethnoarchaeology* (pp. 13–26). Institute of Archaeology, University of California, Los Angeles. (Monograph 4)

Stanislawski, M. (1978). If pots were mortal. In R. Gould (Ed.), *Explorations in Ethnoarchaeology* (pp. 201–228). Albuquerque: University of New Mexico Press.

Steward, J. (1955). *Theory of culture change.* Urbana: University of Illinois Press.

Steward, J. (1968). Cultural ecology. In D. Sills (Ed.), *International encyclopedia of the social sciences: Vol. 4.* (pp. 337–344). New York: Macmillan.

Strong, E. (1959). *Stone age on the Columbia River.* Portland, OR: Binfords and Mort.

Stryd, A. (1973). *The later prehistory of the Lillooet area, British Columbia.* Doctoral dissertation, University of Calgary, Calgary.

Stryd, A., & Rousseau, M. (1995). The early prehistory of the Mid Fraser–Thompson River area. In R. Carlson & L. Dalla Bona (Eds.), *Early human occupation in British Columbia.* Vancouver: University of British Columbia Press.

Teit, J. A. (1900). *The Thompson Indians of British Columbia.* Memoir of the American Museum of Natural History, 2, (4).

Teit, J. A. (1906). *The Lillooet Indians.* Memoir of the American Museum of Natural History, 2, (5).

Teit, J. A. (1909). *The Shuswap.* Memoir of theAmerican Museum of Natural History 2, (7): 447–789.

Teit, J. A. (1912a). *Mythology of the Thompson Indians.* Memoir of the American Museum of Natural History (8): 199–416.

Teit, J. A. (1912b). Traditions of the Lillooet Indians of British Columbia. *Journal of American Folk-Lore, 25,* 287–371.

Teit, J. A. (1917). *Folk-tales of Salishan and Sahaptin tribes.* New York: American Folk-Lore Society.

Testart, A. (1982). The significance of food storage among hunter–gatherers. *Current Anthropology, 23,* 523–537.

Torrence, R. (Ed.). (1989). *Time, energy and stone tools.* Cambridge: University of Cambridge Press.

Turner, N. (1992). Plant resources of the Stl'atl'imx (Fraser River Lillooet) people: A window into the past. In B. Hayden (Ed.), *A complex culture of the British Columbia Plateau* (pp. 405–469). Vancouver: University of British Columbia Press.

Wagner, P. (1960). *The human use of the earth.* Westerville, OH: Glencoe Press.

Whallon, R. (1968). Investigations of late prehistoric social organization in New York State. In S. Binford & L. Binford (Eds.), *New perspectives in archaeology* (pp. 223–244). Chicago: Aldine.

White, L. (1957). *The evolution of culture.* New York: McGraw-Hill.

Wilson, I. R. (1992). *Excavations at the Baker site: EdQx 43, Monte Creek, Permit 91–107.* Report submitted to the Ministry of Transportation and Highways, on file with the Archaeology Branch, British Columbia Provincial Government, Victoria, British Columbia.

CREDITS

Fig. 1.1, 1.2, 2.1 Elizabeth Crowfoot; Fig. 1.3, 1.4, 2.3, 3.4, 7.1, 7.5 Brian Hayden;
Fig. 2.2 A–D, 3.7 (bottom right) Teit 1900, 1906; Fig. 2.2 E, F, 4.5, 5.1 Jaclynne Campbell;
Fig. 2.4 David Cole; Figure 2.5, 3.8 B. Hayden and Jaclynne Campbell; Fig. 3.1 Jon
Murray/The Province; Fig. 3.2 Triathalon Inc. and Elizabeth Crowfoot; Fig. 3.3 Ian Kuijt
and Elizabeth Crowfoot; Fig. 3.5 Diana Alexander and Elizabeth Crowfoot, Richards and
Rousseau (1987), and Stryd and Rousseau (1995); Fig. 3.7 Photo courtesy of the British
Columbia Archives and Records Service. Catalog Number 16465 (A–6160); Fig. 3.9, 5.2,
5.4, 5.5, 5.6 James Spafford (1991); Fig. 4.1 Daniel Holmberg; Fig. 4.1 (top) Robert
Carneiro (1967); Fig. 4.2 (bottom) Reproduced by permission of the American
Anthropological Association from *American Anthropologist* 58, 1956. Not for reproduction,
Fig 4.3 James Spafford, Arnoud Stryd (1973), and Jaclynne Campbell; Fig. 4.4 Rick
Schulting; Fig. 4.6, 7.7 Kevin Berry; Fig. 4.7 Richard MacDonald; Fig. 5.3, 7.3 Martin
Handley, Jaclynne Campbell; Fig. 5.7 Elizabeth Crowfoot and Jaclynne Campbell;
Fig. 6.1 Dana Lepofsky and Jim Spafford; Fig. 6.2, 6.3 William Middleton; Fig. 7.2 Karla
Kusmer and Jim Spafford; Fig. 7.4 David Huelsbeck (1994); Fig. 7.6 Sasha Brown, Dione
McConnachie, and Jaclynne Campbell; Fig. 8.1 Edward Bakewell; Fig. 9.1 Photo courtesy
of the Canadian Museum of Civilization, images number 23212 and 35995.

INDEX

Activity areas, 68
Aggrandizers, 112, 114–118
Animal diversity, 104
Archaic, 8, 11
Architecture, 57
Art, 8, 11

Basketry, 86
Birds, 101, 104–105
Boiling, 8, 92
Bone, jewelry, 101–103
    tools, 103
Burials, 13, 22

Chemistry, soil, *See* Soil chemistry.
Chiefs, *See* Elites.
Competition, 8, 12–13
Complex hunter–gatherers, 1, 7–9, 10–13
    defined, 8, 10
Complexity, 8–9, 49, 102, 111*ff*
Conifer, needles, 78
    posts, 59
Contracts, 112, 114
Copper, 74
Corporate groups, *See* Residential corporate
    groups.
Coyotes, 15, 122–125
Cultural ecology, 1, 11
Cultural evolution, 7–8, 11–12, 111
Curation, tool, 103

Debitage, 65–67
Debt, 112
Dogs, 22, 97–101, 106, 127
Domestication, 8, 86, 101, 106

Elites, 22–23, 71, 107, 115–116
Ethnographic analogy, 16–17, 25, 80

Fats, 20, 92, 95
Feasts, 22–23, 59, 112, 116–118
Fire-cracked rock, 41, 63–64
Firewood, 83
Fishing sites and platforms, 18–19, 90–91
Formation processes, 36–42
    botanical, 78
    faunal, 89–93
    lithic, 61–63
Fraser River, 2
Fraser, Simon, 2

Generalized hunter–gatherers, 11, 12, 49, 118
Gift giving, 112–114
Gini indices, 50–51
Glaciers, 2

Hearths, 51–53
Heating strategies, 46–51
Hierarchies, 13, 25, 50–51, 110–112
Hunter–gatherers, *See* Complex hunter–gatherers,
    Generalized hunter–gatherers.
Hunting, 20, 95

Inheritance, 19, 22–23

Jewelry, 11, 101–102

Lillooet, town, 2
Lorenz curves, 50–51

Mesolithic, 7, 111–112
    definition, 8
Microblades, 6
Middle Prehistoric period, 6
Mobility, *See* Sedentism.
Morgan, Lewis Henry, 6, 104

Neolithic, 8
Nephrite, 73

Ownership, 8, 13, 22, 24, 74–75, 104, 108–110,
    112

Pipes, 74, 86, 116
Planks, wood, 83
Plants, food, 77–79, 80–83
    technology, 83–86
    diversity, 87
Political organization, 22
Polygyny, 19
Population, density, 11–12, 45–47
    site, 47
Postholes, 54–59, 110
Post-Processual archaeology, 9–10
Potlatch, *See* feasts
Prestige objects, 8, 12–13, 73–75, 101–103, 107,
    117
Processual archaeology, 9–10

Ramps, 45
Refuse, deer, 93

fish, 90–95
plant, 83
stone, 64–67
Residential corporate groups, 27, 104, 108–110, 117–119
Resources, 1, 7, 11–12, 18–22, 23–24, 25, 104, 111–113, 118
overexploitation of, 12
ownership of, *See* Ownership.
Roasting pits, 59–60
Roofs, 40–42, 57–58

Sacrifices, dog, 98, 100–101
Salmon, 18, 20, 89–95, 103–105
Sedentism, 11–12
Shamans, 106
Sharing, 12–13, 22
Shells, 101–102
Simple hunter–gatherers, *See* Generalized hunter–gatherers.
Slavery, 7, 13, 22–23, 101
Sleeping areas, 80

Smoking, 86
Social organization, 22
Soil chemistry, 80–82
Status, 113–114
Stone, tools, 61*ff*
sources, 108–110
Storage, food, 8, 11–13, 20, 107, 111
pits, 53–54, 110
tool, 69
Stratification; economic, social, political, 25

Technology, 8, 12, 111
Testing program, 28–34
Trade, 13, 22, 111, 117
Transegalitarian societies, 11, 20, 115–116

Upper Paleolithic, 7, 11, 112

Warfare, 22, 117
Wealth, 22
Wives, 19
Women, 19–20, 23, 68–69